SAN .
ISLANDS
TRAVEL GUIDE

2024 Edition

Discover the Hidden Gems and Richness of Washington's Archipelago

Jim Baxter

TABLE OF CONTENT

Chapter 4: Outdoor Adventures

Kayaking and Boating: Embark on an aquatic adventure, exploring the diverse waterways and wildlife-rich habitats around the islands.

Hiking and Nature Trails: Lace up your boots and traverse the scenic trails, taking you through old-growth forests, coastal bluffs, and panoramic viewpoints.

Whale Watching and Wildlife Encounters: Learn about the best spots to witness majestic orcas, seals, bald eagles, and other fascinating creatures.

Chapter 5: Cultural and Historical Highlights

Art and Galleries: Immerse yourself in the vibrant local arts scene, visiting galleries, studios, and art events that showcase the talent of the islands.

Native American Heritage: Explore the rich history and culture of the Coast Salish people, whose presence in the San Juans dates back thousands of years.

Lighthouses and Historical Sites: Delve into the maritime heritage of the islands, visiting historic lighthouses, museums, and preserved landmarks.

Chapter 6: Dining, Shopping, and Accommodations

Culinary Delights: Indulge in farm-to-table cuisine, seafood delicacies, and local specialties at the island's diverse restaurants and eateries.

Unique Shopping Experiences: Discover charming boutiques, art galleries, and local markets, offering one-of-a-kind souvenirs and handmade goods.

Accommodation Options: From cozy bed and breakfasts to waterfront resorts, find the perfect place to stay during your San Juan Islands getaway.

Chapter 7: Planning and Resources

Important Notice Before You continue Reading!!!

Step into the pages of this travel guide and prepare for a truly extraordinary experience. Delve into the captivating world of San Juan Islands, where imagination, creativity, and a thirst for adventure reign supreme. You won't find any images within these pages, as we firmly believe in the power of firsthand exploration, devoid of visual filters or preconceptions. Each monument, every nook and cranny eagerly awaits your arrival, ready to astonish and amaze. Why spoil the thrill of that initial glimpse, that overwhelming sense of wonder? So get ready to embark on an unparalleled journey, where your imagination becomes the sole means of transportation and you, the ultimate guide. Release any preconceived notions and allow yourself to be transported to an authentic San Juan Islands brimming with hidden treasures. Let the enchantment commence, but remember, the most breathtaking images will be the ones painted by your own eyes.

Unlike many conventional guides, this book needs no detailed maps. Why, you may ask? Because we firmly believe that the truest discoveries happen when you wander, when you surrender to the current of the surroundings and embrace the uncertainty of the path. No rigid itineraries or precise directions are provided here, for we yearn for you to explore San Juan Islands on your own terms, unbound by limitations or restrictions. Surrender yourself to the currents and unearth hidden gems that no map could reveal. Be audacious, follow your instincts, and brace yourself for serendipitous encounters. The magic of the journey commences now, within a world without maps, where roads materialize with each step and the most extraordinary adventures await in the folds of the unknown.

Chapter 1: Introduction to the San Juan Islands

Welcome to the San Juan Islands: A brief overview of the archipelago's geography, history, and cultural significance.

Nestled in the Salish Sea, off the northwest coast of Washington state, lies the enchanting San Juan Islands. This picturesque archipelago is a hidden gem that captures the hearts of visitors from around the world. Composed of approximately 172 named islands and reefs, with Orcas Island, San Juan Island, Lopez Island, and Shaw Island as the main attractions, the San Juans offer a unique blend of natural beauty, rich history, and a vibrant island culture.

The geography of the San Juan Islands is a testament to the awe-inspiring forces of nature. Formed by glacial activity during the last ice age, the landscape showcases deep fjords, rugged shorelines, and dramatic cliffs that stand tall against the crashing waves. The islands are a haven for nature enthusiasts and adventure seekers alike, with lush forests covering the land and providing habitats for a diverse range of wildlife. Exploring the islands, you may encounter deer grazing in meadows, bald eagles soaring overhead, and seals basking on rocky outcrops. The islands also offer breathtaking vistas, with sweeping views of the surrounding sea and the snow-capped peaks of the Olympic and Cascade mountain ranges in the distance.

The San Juan Islands have a rich history that is deeply intertwined with various cultures. For thousands of years, the Coast Salish people have inhabited the region and have a profound connection to the islands. These indigenous communities have left their mark through traditional stories, intricate art, and the preservation of sacred sites. Exploring the islands allows visitors to gain a deeper understanding of the indigenous heritage that continues to thrive in the region. You can learn about the ancient legends and spiritual practices that are still passed down through generations, and appreciate the resilience and wisdom of the Coast Salish people.

European exploration of the San Juan Islands began in the late 18th century, as Spanish and British navigators set their sights on the region. The archipelago became a point of contention between these two colonial powers, each seeking control of the area for its strategic importance in the fur trade and maritime routes. The dispute over the boundary between the United States and Britain reached its peak in 1859 when the infamous Pig War erupted. The conflict was sparked by an incident where an American settler shot a pig owned by a British farmer. Though the conflict never escalated to actual combat, both sides established military presence on the islands. Ultimately, the dispute was resolved through arbitration, and the San Juan Islands became part of the United States. The remnants of this historical event can still be explored today, with preserved military installations and interpretive sites providing glimpses into the past.

Present-day San Juan Islands are known for their tranquil and laid-back atmosphere. The tight-knit island communities have fostered a unique island culture that celebrates local arts, sustainable living, and a deep connection to nature. Artists from various disciplines are drawn to the islands' serene beauty, finding inspiration in the landscapes and the sense of community. The islands also have a thriving farming community, with local farmers cultivating an array of fresh produce, including berries, vegetables, and artisanal cheeses. Farmers' markets showcase these local delights, allowing visitors to savor the flavors of the islands. Sustainable living practices are embraced by many residents, with a focus on renewable energy, conservation, and environmentally conscious initiatives. This commitment to preserving the natural beauty of the islands ensures that future generations can continue to experience the San Juans' wonders.

The sense of community in the San Juan Islands is palpable, with locals warmly welcoming visitors and sharing their love for the islands' natural wonders. Whether you choose to explore the charming town of Eastsound on Orcas Island, wander the historic streets of Friday Harbor on San Juan Island, or relax on the serene beaches of Lopez Island, you will be embraced by the island's welcoming spirit. The islands offer a plethora of activities, including kayaking, whale watching, hiking, and beachcombing, ensuring there is something for everyone to enjoy.

In the San Juan Islands, time slows down, and you'll find yourself immersed in the captivating beauty of nature, enveloped by the islands' rich history, and embraced by the warmth of the island communities. A visit to the San Juans is an experience that will leave an indelible mark on your heart and a desire to return to this magical archipelago time and time again.

Getting There and Getting Around: Essential information on transportation options, including ferry services, flights, and inter-island transportation.

Reaching the San Juan Islands is part of the adventure. The most common mode of transportation is by ferry, which adds to the sense of anticipation as you embark on your island journey. The Washington State Ferries operate regular routes to the San Juans from Anacortes, located on the mainland. The ferry ride itself is a scenic experience, offering breathtaking views of the surrounding waterways and the possibility of spotting marine wildlife along the way.

The journey from Anacortes to the San Juan Islands is a highlight for many visitors. As you board the ferry, you can feel the excitement in the air as fellow travelers eagerly anticipate their island getaway. The vessels are spacious and comfortable, with indoor and outdoor seating options. Whether you choose to relax inside and enjoy the views from large windows or venture to the open decks for an immersive experience, the ferry ride sets the stage for the natural wonders that await.

As the ferry navigates through the Salish Sea, you'll be treated to stunning panoramas of emerald green islands, rugged coastlines, and snow-capped mountains in the distance. Keep your eyes peeled for marine wildlife that call these waters home. Orcas, also known as killer whales, are a common sight, gracefully swimming alongside the ferry. Seals, sea lions, and porpoises may also make an appearance, adding to the excitement of the journey.

For those preferring a quicker and more direct option, seaplane and air taxi services are available from several locations, including Seattle and Bellingham. These flights offer a bird's-eye view of the islands and allow for convenient access to your destination. The seaplanes take off and land on the water, providing a unique and exhilarating experience. As you soar above the islands, you'll gain a new perspective of their beauty, with aerial vistas showcasing the intricate network of islands, the turquoise waters, and the lush forests that cover the land.

Private boat charters and marinas are also available for those who wish to explore the islands at their own pace. If you have boating experience or choose to hire a captain, you can navigate the waterways surrounding the San Juan Islands, anchoring in secluded coves and exploring hidden beaches. This option provides the ultimate freedom and flexibility, allowing you to discover remote corners of the archipelago that are inaccessible by other means of transportation.

Once you've arrived in the San Juans, getting around the islands is a breeze. The most common mode of transportation on the islands is by car, which allows for easy exploration and access to the various attractions. Rental cars are available on Orcas, San Juan, and Lopez Islands, offering visitors the freedom to roam and discover hidden gems at their leisure.

Having a car provides the convenience of being able to explore the islands on your own schedule. It allows you to navigate the winding roads that lead to scenic viewpoints, stunning beaches, and charming towns. You can embark on a leisurely drive along the coast, stopping at viewpoints to soak in the breathtaking scenery. Plus, having a car enables you to carry any outdoor gear or picnic supplies you may need for your adventures.

However, for a more leisurely and environmentally-friendly experience, consider renting a bicycle. The San Juan Islands are known for their bike-friendly roads and scenic trails, making cycling an ideal way to immerse yourself in the natural beauty and slower pace of island life. Several rental shops offer a variety of bikes, including electric-assist bicycles for those seeking a little extra boost.

Cycling on the San Juan Islands allows you to connect with the environment and truly appreciate the sights, sounds, and scents of the islands. Pedal at your own pace as you traverse quiet roads lined with picturesque farmlands, rolling hills, and breathtaking coastal vistas. Discover hidden beaches, stop by local farm stands to sample fresh produce, and explore charming waterfront towns—all while reducing your carbon footprint.

Inter-island transportation is also available for island hopping. The Washington State Ferries offer regular service between Orcas, San Juan, and Lopez Islands, allowing you to easily explore multiple destinations during your visit. These inter-island ferries provide a convenient and scenic mode of transportation, connecting the islands and offering a different perspective of the archipelago from the water.

In addition to the Washington State Ferries, private water taxis and charters provide convenient and flexible transportation between the islands, making it possible to create your own custom itinerary. These private services offer personalized experiences, allowing you to customize your island-hopping adventure. Whether you're traveling with a group of friends or seeking a romantic getaway, private charters can cater to your needs, taking you to the hidden gems and lesser-known spots that make the San Juan Islands truly special.

No matter which mode of transportation you choose, getting around the San Juan Islands is an enjoyable part of the journey. Each option offers its own unique experience, whether it's the anticipation of a ferry ride, the thrill of a seaplane flight, the freedom of driving, the tranquility of cycling, or the convenience of island-hopping via inter-island ferries or private charters. Embrace the adventure and take in the beauty of the San Juan Islands as you embark on your exploration of this captivating archipelago.

When to Visit: A seasonal guide to help you plan your trip based on weather, wildlife sightings, and popular events.

The San Juan Islands offer a unique experience in every season, each with its own distinct charm. To help you plan your trip, here's a seasonal guide highlighting the key features of each time of year:

Spring (March to May):

As winter retreats and the days grow longer, the San Juan Islands burst into life during the spring season. The islands awaken from their winter slumber, and vibrant colors start to dot the landscape as wildflowers bloom in meadows and along trails. The air is filled with the sweet fragrance of blossoms, creating a delightful sensory experience.

Spring is a fantastic time for birdwatching enthusiasts. Migratory birds return to the islands, seeking refuge and abundant food sources. Bald eagles, with their majestic wingspans, can be spotted soaring through the skies. Graceful herons wade in the shallows, patiently hunting for fish. The islands also become a chorus of songbirds, with their melodic tunes echoing through the trees. Binoculars in hand, you can explore the various birding hotspots, such as Lime Kiln Point State Park and the National Wildlife Refuges.

One of the highlights of spring in the San Juan Islands is the opportunity to witness the incredible migration of gray whales. These magnificent marine mammals make their way along the coast, passing through the waters of the Salish Sea. Keep your eyes peeled for the telltale spouts and graceful breaches as these gentle giants make their journey northwards. Excursions are available for whale watching, allowing you to observe these majestic creatures up close while learning about their behaviors and conservation efforts.

In addition to birdwatching and whale watching, the San Juan Islands offer ample chances to encounter other marine wildlife. Seals, sea lions, and playful otters frequent the shores and harbors, basking in the warm spring sunshine. Keep an eye out for their curious heads popping out of the water or catching a glimpse of them sunning themselves on rocks. Kayaking or taking a boat tour provides a unique vantage point to observe these fascinating creatures in their natural habitat.

Spring is also a time of celebration for the local community. The islands come alive with charming farmer's markets, where you can browse stalls filled with fresh produce, artisanal crafts, and homemade treats. These markets offer a wonderful opportunity to connect with the islanders, taste the flavors of the region, and support local businesses. Immerse yourself in the island's agricultural bounty as you sample farm-fresh berries, indulge in handmade chocolates, and savor locally produced cheeses.

The arrival of spring is marked by lively local festivals that showcase the vibrant island culture. From the Orcas Island Lit Fest, a gathering of renowned authors and book lovers, to the Lopez Island Artists Studio Tour, where you can explore the private studios of talented artists, there's something for every artistic inclination. Music enthusiasts can revel in the Orcas Island Chamber Music Festival, featuring world-class performances in breathtaking island venues.

Summer (June to August):

With the arrival of summer, the San Juan Islands enter their peak tourism season. The weather is generally sunny and mild, creating the perfect conditions for outdoor activities and exploration. The islands are ablaze with color, with blooming flowers, lush greenery, and sparkling blue waters that invite you to indulge in the beauty of nature.

The San Juans are renowned for their abundant marine wildlife, and summer provides an excellent opportunity to witness these creatures in their natural habitat. Orca whales, the iconic symbols of the islands, are frequently spotted during this season. These magnificent creatures, with their distinctive black and white markings, captivate visitors with their graceful presence and playful behaviors. Humpback whales and minke whales also make appearances, adding to the excitement of a whale watching excursion.

The islands become a playground for outdoor enthusiasts during the summer months. Kayaking is a popular activity, allowing you to paddle through the calm and clear waters, exploring hidden coves, and observing marine life up close. Rent a kayak or join a guided tour to venture to picturesque spots like Sucia Island or the intricate waterways of the Salish Sea.

Boating enthusiasts can set sail on their own adventures, cruising between the islands and discovering secluded anchorages. The San Juan Islands offer excellent facilities for boaters, with numerous marinas, public docks, and mooring buoys available. Whether you're an experienced sailor or a novice looking to try your hand at navigating the pristine waters, the islands offer endless possibilities for exploration.

For those who prefer to keep their feet on land, hiking is a wonderful way to experience the natural beauty of the San Juan Islands. Miles of trails wind through forests, along rugged coastlines, and up scenic hills, offering breathtaking views at every turn. Orcas Island, with its diverse topography, boasts a variety of trails suitable for all levels of hikers. Mount Constitution, the highest point in the San Juan Islands, rewards hikers with panoramic vistas of the surrounding islands and waterways.

Summer also brings a vibrant arts and cultural scene to the San Juan Islands. The islands come alive with various events and festivals that showcase the talent and creativity of the local community. Art shows feature works from local artists and artisans, displaying a wide range of mediums, including painting, sculpture, ceramics, and jewelry. Music performances, from classical concerts to lively outdoor gigs, fill the air with melodies that harmonize with the natural surroundings.

The Orcas Island Chamber Music Festival is a highlight of the summer cultural calendar. This internationally acclaimed festival brings world-class musicians to the islands, performing in stunning venues such as the Rosario Resort's historic Music Room. Immerse yourself in the transcendent sounds of classical music, as the melodies blend with the serenity of the island landscapes.

Fall (September to November):

As summer transitions into fall, the San Juan Islands transform into a tranquil oasis. The crowds disperse, and a peaceful ambiance settles over the archipelago. The changing colors of the foliage create a breathtaking backdrop for scenic hikes and drives, with vibrant hues of red, orange, and gold painting the landscapes.

Fall marks an important event in the natural cycle of the San Juan Islands—the return of salmon. September is when these resilient fish embark on their annual spawning journey, navigating the island's rivers and streams. The arrival of salmon attracts orcas, seals, and sea lions, who feast on the abundant food source. Witnessing the spectacle of an orca pod chasing and capturing salmon is a thrilling experience that highlights the intricate balance of the marine ecosystem.

This season is perfect for embarking on scenic hikes, immersing yourself in the tranquility of nature, and relishing the solitude of the trails. Moran State Park on Orcas Island offers an extensive network of trails that wind through old-growth forests and around pristine lakes. The trails are especially enchanting during fall, with the fallen leaves creating a carpet of color underfoot.

Fall is also a time of harvest festivals in the San Juan Islands. Local farms and vineyards celebrate the bounty of the season, showcasing the region's agricultural riches. From pumpkin patches to apple orchards, you can partake in the time-honored tradition of picking your own produce straight from the fields. Savor the flavors of freshly harvested fruits and vegetables, indulge in homemade pies and cider, and experience the authentic taste of island-grown goodness.

Culinary delights await at the fall harvest festivals, where local chefs and artisans come together to create delectable dishes that highlight the seasonal ingredients. The islands' farm-to-table ethos is showcased through farm dinners and tasting events, where you can enjoy expertly prepared meals that showcase the flavors of the region. It's an opportunity to savor the terroir of the islands and appreciate the dedication of the farmers and food producers who contribute to the vibrant culinary scene.

Winter (December to February):

Winter in the San Juans offers a quiet and serene escape from the hustle and bustle of daily life. The islands take on a more secluded and intimate atmosphere, allowing for peaceful reflection and rejuvenation. The crisp air invigorates the senses, and the absence of summer crowds enhances the feeling of solitude.

Storm watching is a popular activity during the winter months, as the San Juan Islands experience the power and drama of the Pacific Northwest weather. The crashing waves, swirling mists, and dramatic skies create a mesmerizing spectacle that showcases the raw beauty of nature. Find a cozy spot by the window in a waterfront cabin or visit a seaside café to watch the storms unfold, listening to the rhythmic sounds of the waves crashing against the rocky shores.

Despite the cooler temperatures, winter continues to offer opportunities for wildlife encounters. Gray whales can still be spotted during their migration along the coast, delighting those who venture out on whale watching excursions. Binoculars in hand, scan the horizon for the telltale spouts and graceful breaches of these gentle giants. Birdwatching enthusiasts can take advantage of the absence of leaves on trees, which provides better visibility for observing a variety of avian species.

Winter is also a time for cultural exploration in the San Juan Islands. The islands boast a rich history and a vibrant arts scene that can be experienced year-round. Museums, art galleries, and historical sites offer insights into the islands' past and present. Take a stroll through the historic downtown areas, where charming boutiques, cozy cafés, and art studios beckon with their warmth and creativity.

The San Juan Islands' close-knit community embraces the winter season with a variety of events and gatherings. Holiday festivities light up the islands, with tree lighting ceremonies, craft fairs, and seasonal markets. Celebrate the local culture and traditions by attending concerts, theater performances, and community gatherings that bring people together in the spirit of warmth and camaraderie.

Regardless of the season you choose to visit, it's important to note that weather in the Pacific Northwest can be unpredictable. Dressing in layers, carrying a waterproof jacket, and being prepared for changes in weather are essential. The beauty of the San Juan Islands transcends the seasons, offering a captivating experience that will leave you with cherished memories of your island adventure, no matter the time of year.

Chapter 2: Exploring the Major Islands

Orcas Island: Dive into the largest island of the San Juans, known for its lush forests, charming villages, and stunning Moran State Park.

Natural Beauty and Outdoor Adventures:

Moran State Park:

Located on Orcas Island, Moran State Park is a nature lover's paradise, encompassing over 5,000 acres of pristine wilderness. With its diverse landscapes, picturesque hiking trails, serene lakes, and stunning viewpoints, the park offers a myriad of opportunities for outdoor adventures and breathtaking experiences.

Exploring the Hiking Trails:

Moran State Park boasts a network of well-maintained hiking trails that cater to all skill levels. Whether you're a seasoned hiker or a casual nature enthusiast, there's a trail for everyone to enjoy. One popular trail is the Mount Constitution Trail, which leads to the summit of Mount Constitution, the highest point in the San Juan Islands. As you ascend through the forested slopes, you'll be rewarded with sweeping vistas of the surrounding islands and waterways. On a clear day, you can even catch a glimpse of the majestic Olympic Mountains to the south and the Canadian Gulf Islands to the north.

For a more leisurely hike, the Cascade Falls Trail is an excellent choice. This trail takes you through moss-covered old-growth forests, passing by the mesmerizing Cascade Falls along the way. The sound of rushing water and the lush greenery create a tranquil and rejuvenating ambiance.

Serene Lakes and Water Activities:

Within Moran State Park, there are several lakes that offer opportunities for swimming, boating, and picnicking. Cascade Lake, the largest lake in the park, is a haven of tranquility. Its calm, crystal-clear waters invite visitors to take a refreshing dip or leisurely paddle in a kayak or canoe. As you glide across the surface, surrounded by the scenic beauty of the park, you'll feel a deep sense of peace and connection with nature. The lake's sandy beaches are perfect for spreading out a picnic blanket and enjoying a meal amidst the idyllic surroundings.

Wildlife and Nature Observation:

Moran State Park is teeming with wildlife, making it a prime spot for nature enthusiasts and birdwatchers. Keep an eye out for the park's diverse bird species, including bald eagles, great blue herons, and various songbirds. You may also spot deer and other small mammals along the trails, as they go about their daily routines in harmony with the natural environment. Take a moment to appreciate the delicate balance of ecosystems and the interconnectedness of all living beings.

Historic Landmarks:

While exploring Moran State Park, you'll come across a few historic landmarks that add to its charm and significance. One notable landmark is the stone observation tower atop Mount Constitution. Built by the Civilian Conservation Corps during the Great Depression, the tower offers a panoramic view that stretches as far as the eye can see. It's a testament to the rich history of the park and the dedication of those who worked to preserve its natural beauty.

Cultural and Recreational Facilities:

To enhance visitors' experiences, Moran State Park offers various amenities and recreational facilities. The park features picnic areas with tables and grills, providing the perfect setting for a family gathering or a leisurely lunch in nature. Campgrounds are available for those who wish to extend their stay and immerse themselves fully in the park's serene ambiance. Additionally, the park offers opportunities for horseback riding, mountain biking, and even disc golf, ensuring there's always something for everyone to enjoy.

Anecdote:

As you hike along the trails of Moran State Park, you may come across an enchanting encounter with the park's resident wildlife. Imagine walking through a dense forest, the sunlight filtering through the towering trees. Suddenly, a majestic bald eagle soars above you, its wings outstretched against the azure sky. It circles effortlessly, scanning the landscape below. You pause, captivated by the beauty and grace of this iconic bird, as it serves as a reminder of the park's role in preserving the natural habitat for such magnificent creatures.

Example:

One of the most memorable experiences in Moran State Park is hiking to the summit of Mount Constitution. The trail winds its way through a mix of towering conifers, lush ferns, and vibrant wildflowers, creating a sensory feast for the avid nature lover. Along the journey, you might encounter a variety of wildlife, such as deer grazing in the meadows or a playful squirrel darting across the path. As you ascend higher, the air becomes crisper, and the views become more expansive.

Reaching the top of Mount Constitution is a triumph, rewarded by a breathtaking panoramic view that stretches in all directions. You stand in awe as you gaze out over the surrounding islands, their emerald forests meeting the deep blue waters of the Salish Sea. On a clear day, the distant peaks of the Olympic Mountains stand majestically to the south, a reminder of the vastness and grandeur of the natural world.

While descending from Mount Constitution, you may decide to take a detour to Cascade Lake. The path meanders through a serene forest, the sound of birdsong accompanying your every step. As you approach the lake, you catch glimpses of sunlight sparkling on the water's surface through gaps in the trees. The inviting sight draws you closer, and soon you find yourself on the sandy beach, taking off your shoes and dipping your toes into the refreshing water. Time seems to stand still as you bask in the peaceful atmosphere, surrounded by the symphony of nature.

Moran State Park and its various attractions, from the majestic Mount Constitution to the tranquil Cascade Lake, provide an immersive experience in the beauty and tranquility of the San Juan Islands. Whether you're seeking adventure on the hiking trails, relaxation by the lakeside, or a connection with the natural world, Moran State Park offers a sanctuary for the soul and an opportunity to create lifelong memories.

Turtleback Mountain Preserve:

Turtleback Mountain Preserve: Embark on a scenic hike through diverse ecosystems, including forests, meadows, and rocky cliffs, while enjoying panoramic views of the surrounding islands and waterways.

Located on the western side of Orcas Island, Turtleback Mountain Preserve is a true gem within the San Juan Islands archipelago. This 1,578-acre preserve offers a variety of hiking trails that wind through lush forests, open meadows, and rugged cliffs, providing visitors with an unforgettable experience of the island's natural beauty.

As you set foot on the trails of Turtleback Mountain Preserve, you'll immediately be captivated by the tranquility and serenity of the surroundings. The preserve is home to a remarkable array of flora and fauna, making it a haven for nature enthusiasts and wildlife observers. The trails meander through old-growth forests, where towering Douglas firs and western red cedars create a verdant canopy overhead. Keep an eye out for moss-covered logs, delicate wildflowers, and the sweet scent of the forest that fills the air.

One of the most popular hikes within the preserve is the Turtleback Mountain Trail, a moderate 3.6-mile loop that leads you to the summit of Turtleback Mountain itself. As you ascend, you'll encounter breathtaking panoramic views of the surrounding islands, including Shaw Island, Crane Island, and the snow-capped peaks of the Olympic Mountains in the distance. On clear days, Mount Baker stands tall on the horizon, adding to the awe-inspiring vista.

The trail ascends through forests filled with native plant species such as sword ferns, salal bushes, and Oregon grape. As you reach higher elevations, the landscape transitions to rocky outcrops and open meadows, offering glimpses of wildlife that call this area home. Keep your eyes peeled for deer grazing in the fields, eagles soaring overhead, and, if you're lucky, the occasional sighting of a majestic red fox or elusive black-tailed deer.

As you continue along the trail, you'll come across viewpoints that invite you to pause and soak in the natural beauty around you. The San Juan Islands stretch out before you like a painter's canvas, with sparkling blue waters, dense evergreen forests, and rocky shorelines creating a stunning panorama. These moments of reflection and connection with nature are what make the Turtleback Mountain Preserve hike so special.

For those seeking a longer adventure, the preserve offers additional trails that traverse different sections of the island. The South Trail, for example, takes you on a 7.3-mile loop through diverse ecosystems, including wetlands, forests, and grassy meadows. This trail provides opportunities to spot a wide variety of bird species, such as great blue herons, kingfishers, and woodpeckers. The West Boundary Trail, on the other hand, leads you along the western edge of the preserve, offering glimpses of rocky cliffs, sandy beaches, and breathtaking sunsets.

Beyond its natural beauty, Turtleback Mountain Preserve holds historical and cultural significance as well. The mountain and surrounding lands were acquired by the San Juan County Land Bank in 2006, thanks to a community-led conservation effort that aimed to protect the area from development and preserve it for future generations. This collaboration between local residents, conservation organizations, and the land bank showcases the deep connection that the island community has with its natural environment.

Before embarking on your hike, it's recommended to stop by the Turtleback Mountain Preserve trailhead and visitor center, located on Crow Valley Road. Here, you can pick up trail maps, get information on current trail conditions, and learn about the history and ecology of the preserve. The visitor center also serves as a gathering place for local volunteers and hikers, creating a sense of community and shared stewardship of this beautiful natural space.

When planning your visit to Turtleback Mountain Preserve, it's important to come prepared. Wear sturdy footwear suitable for hiking, and dress in layers to accommodate changes in temperature and weather conditions. Carry plenty of water and snacks, as there are no facilities within the preserve itself. Additionally, remember to practice Leave No Trace principles, respecting the delicate balance of the ecosystem and ensuring the preservation of this remarkable place for future generations.

Turtleback Mountain Preserve is not only a place for outdoor recreation but also an opportunity to connect with the awe-inspiring beauty and tranquility of Orcas Island. The diverse ecosystems, breathtaking vistas, and rich biodiversity make this preserve a must-visit destination for nature enthusiasts and hikers alike. Whether you choose to embark on a leisurely stroll through the forests or challenge yourself with a summit hike, Turtleback Mountain Preserve promises an unforgettable experience that will leave you with a profound appreciation for the natural wonders of the San Juan Islands.

Cascade Lake:

Nestled in the heart of Orcas Island, Cascade Lake is a picturesque oasis that beckons visitors with its serene ambiance and natural splendor. Surrounded by lush forests and towering evergreen trees, this pristine lake offers a tranquil retreat for those seeking relaxation, outdoor activities, and a chance to immerse themselves in the island's breathtaking beauty.

As you approach Cascade Lake, you'll be greeted by the calming sound of water cascading down a small waterfall, adding to the enchanting atmosphere. The lake itself spans over 60 acres, providing ample space for various recreational pursuits. One of the main draws of Cascade Lake is its inviting waters, which are ideal for swimming and cooling off on warm summer days. The lake boasts crystal-clear water that reflects the vibrant colors of the surrounding vegetation, creating a mesmerizing sight that is both soothing and invigorating.

A popular activity at Cascade Lake is picnicking, as numerous picnic tables and grassy areas are scattered along the lakeshore. Whether you're looking to enjoy a quiet, intimate picnic for two or a lively gathering with friends and family, there are plenty of spots to spread out a blanket, set up a picnic basket, and savor a delicious meal amidst nature's embrace. The tranquil ambiance and idyllic setting make Cascade Lake an ideal spot for creating lasting memories and engaging in meaningful conversations.

For those seeking a bit more adventure, Cascade Lake offers opportunities for kayaking and canoeing. Glide across the calm waters, exploring the lake's nooks and crannies, and reveling in the peacefulness of the surroundings. Renting a kayak or canoe from a local outfitter allows you to fully experience the tranquility of Cascade Lake while embracing the sense of freedom that comes with paddling through pristine waters. As you navigate the lake, keep an eye out for the resident wildlife, including ducks, geese, and possibly even a great blue heron gracefully wading along the shore.

Surrounding Cascade Lake is a network of walking trails that meander through the surrounding forests, offering scenic vistas and opportunities to spot native flora and fauna. The trails cater to various skill levels, ranging from easy strolls to more challenging hikes, ensuring that everyone can find a route that suits their preferences. As you venture along these trails, you'll be greeted by towering trees, including Douglas firs, western red cedars, and western hemlocks, which provide shade and create a sense of tranquility as you wander deeper into the woods.

One notable trail near Cascade Lake is the Cascade Falls Trail, a short and relatively easy hike that leads to a captivating waterfall. The trail winds through old-growth forest, with dappled sunlight filtering through the canopy overhead, creating a magical ambiance. As you approach the falls, the sound of rushing water grows louder, building anticipation for the sight that awaits you. Finally, you reach a viewing platform where you can admire the majestic cascade as it plunges into a rocky pool below. The sheer power and natural beauty of the waterfall are awe-inspiring, leaving visitors with a profound appreciation for the wonders of the island.

Cascade Lake is not just a natural retreat; it also holds cultural and historical significance for the local community. It has long been a beloved destination for Orcas Island residents and visitors alike, providing a space for leisure, reflection, and connection with nature. Many generations have forged cherished memories at Cascade Lake, from childhood adventures to romantic escapades and family gatherings. The lake holds a special place in the hearts of the island's inhabitants and serves as a reminder of the island's timeless beauty and enduring spirit.

When planning your visit to Cascade Lake, it's essential to come prepared. Pack a picnic basket filled with delicious local treats, refreshing beverages, and comfortable blankets or chairs to enhance your experience. If you're planning to swim, don't forget to bring your swimsuit, towels, and sunscreen to fully enjoy the pristine waters. Additionally, consider bringing binoculars or a camera to capture the wildlife and stunning landscapes you may encounter during your time at the lake.

Cascade Lake is a hidden gem on Orcas Island, offering a sanctuary of tranquility and natural beauty. Whether you choose to relax by the water's edge, embark on a paddling adventure, or explore the surrounding trails, Cascade Lake invites you to slow down, reconnect with nature, and create unforgettable memories in the heart of the San Juan Islands.

Quaint Villages and Artistic Expression:

Eastsound: Discover the heart of Orcas Island, a charming village filled with unique shops, art galleries, and a vibrant local food scene. Stroll along the waterfront, browse the boutiques, and indulge in farm-to-table dining experiences.

Nestled on the eastern side of Orcas Island, the village of Eastsound beckons visitors with its undeniable charm and captivating ambiance. As you wander through its streets, you'll be greeted by a delightful blend of local businesses, art galleries, and culinary delights that showcase the island's vibrant spirit.

One of the highlights of Eastsound is its picturesque waterfront area. Take a leisurely stroll along the shoreline, where you can enjoy panoramic views of the sparkling waters and the distant peaks of neighboring islands. The gentle lapping of the waves and the scent of the sea create a serene atmosphere that invites you to relax and immerse yourself in the island's natural beauty.

As you explore the village, you'll find a plethora of unique shops offering a diverse range of merchandise. From handmade crafts to locally designed clothing, each boutique exudes its own character, reflecting the creativity and craftsmanship of Orcas Island's artisans. You might stumble upon one-of-a-kind jewelry, handcrafted pottery, or beautifully woven textiles that serve as timeless mementos of your visit.

Art enthusiasts will be captivated by the numerous galleries that dot the streets of Eastsound. Step into these creative spaces, where you can admire works by local painters, sculptors, and photographers. The artistic expression of Orcas Island's community is vibrant and diverse, reflecting the natural landscapes, wildlife, and cultural influences that shape the island's identity. Engage in conversations with the artists themselves, gaining insights into their inspirations and creative processes.

After working up an appetite, Eastsound offers a plethora of dining options that cater to a range of palates. The village has earned a reputation for its farm-to-table culinary scene, where locally sourced ingredients take center stage. Indulge in delectable seafood caught fresh from the surrounding waters, savor artisanal cheeses made by local dairies, or relish in the flavors of seasonal produce harvested from nearby farms. Restaurants and cafes in Eastsound pride themselves on providing a dining experience that is not only delicious but also showcases the region's bountiful resources.

To truly appreciate the farm-to-table concept, consider visiting the weekly farmers' market in Eastsound. Held during the summer months, the market brings together local farmers, artisans, and food vendors, creating a vibrant hub of activity. Here, you can peruse a colorful array of organic fruits and vegetables, taste artisan bread, sample handcrafted cheeses, and discover unique products like wildflower honey and lavender-infused delicacies. Engaging with the local producers provides a deeper understanding of the island's agricultural heritage and the commitment to sustainable practices that underpin the community.

For those with a penchant for history, the Orcas Island Historical Museum offers a fascinating glimpse into the island's past. Housed in a restored strawberry barreling plant, the museum showcases exhibits that span from the indigenous inhabitants to the present day. Immerse yourself in the island's rich history through artifacts, photographs, and engaging narratives that depict the island's evolution and cultural heritage. Discover the stories of early settlers, the development of industries such as logging and fishing, and the traditions and celebrations that have shaped the island's community spirit.

The museum also highlights the unique aspects of Orcas Island's history, such as the Orcas Island Historical Society's collection of historical photographs. These captivating images provide a window into the island's past, showcasing the early days of the village, the bustling waterfront, and the lives of the people who have called Orcas Island home throughout the years. From the archival photographs of bustling wharves to the preserved artifacts of daily life, the museum offers a tangible connection to the island's heritage.

As you explore the exhibits, you might stumble upon intriguing stories and anecdotes that bring the island's history to life. Discover the tales of the island's early schools and the challenges faced by educators in a remote island setting. Learn about the notorious prohibition era and the hidden speakeasies that operated beneath the watchful eye of authorities. These anecdotes offer a glimpse into the unique experiences and colorful characters that have shaped Orcas Island's narrative.

The Orcas Island Historical Museum also hosts special events and educational programs, allowing visitors to engage further with the island's history. From lectures and workshops to guided tours and hands-on activities, these offerings provide an enriching experience that deepens your understanding and appreciation of the island's cultural heritage.

Whether you are captivated by the allure of local art, the flavors of farm-to-table cuisine, or the stories of the island's past, Eastsound and the Orcas Island Historical Museum offer a captivating journey into the heart and soul of Orcas Island. As you soak in the village's charm, you'll leave with a deeper appreciation for the unique blend of creativity, history, and community that define this enchanting destination.

San Juan Island: Discover the bustling town of Friday Harbor, historic sites like English Camp and American Camp, and the iconic Lime Kiln Point State Park.

Historic Sites and Cultural Attractions:

English Camp: Step back in time and explore the remnants of the 19th-century British military encampment. Learn about the Pig War and the island's unique history through guided tours and interpretive exhibits.

Nestled on the scenic San Juan Island, English Camp is a captivating historical site that takes visitors on a journey back in time to the mid-1800s. The camp's intriguing history is rooted in the Pig War, a peaceful standoff between the United States and Great Britain over the disputed boundary between their territories. Today, English Camp stands as a testament to the fascinating events that unfolded during this period.

Upon arriving at English Camp, visitors are greeted by a serene landscape adorned with meadows, towering trees, and remnants of the once-thriving encampment. The camp's historic buildings and structures have been meticulously preserved, offering a glimpse into the daily lives of the British soldiers who occupied the area.

One of the highlights of a visit to English Camp is the opportunity to join a guided tour led by knowledgeable interpreters who bring the history to life. As you explore the camp, you'll hear stories and anecdotes about the soldiers' experiences, the interactions between the British and American forces, and the daily routines that took place within the camp's boundaries.

The interpretive exhibits provide further context and insights into the Pig War and the historical significance of English Camp. Visitors can immerse themselves in the period through artifacts, maps, and informative displays that depict the geopolitical tensions and the diplomatic negotiations that ultimately led to a peaceful resolution.

One notable feature of English Camp is the formal garden, which has been carefully restored to its 19th-century design. Strolling through the garden, you'll discover an array of vibrant flowers, meticulously manicured hedges, and a tranquil atmosphere that transports you to a bygone era.

The natural surroundings of English Camp also offer opportunities for outdoor exploration. A network of hiking trails winds through the area, allowing visitors to meander through the beautiful forested landscape and enjoy the sights and sounds of nature. Keep an eye out for wildlife, including deer, bald eagles, and various species of birds that call the island home.

American Camp: Visit the former U.S. Army encampment and gain insights into the joint military occupation that occurred during the Pig War. Explore the well-preserved barracks and officers' quarters, and enjoy panoramic views of the coastline.

Situated on the southern end of San Juan Island, American Camp provides a captivating counterpart to its British counterpart, English Camp. This former U.S. Army encampment offers a deeper understanding of the joint military occupation and the events that unfolded during the Pig War.

Upon arrival at American Camp, visitors are greeted by rolling prairies, rugged cliffs, and breathtaking views of the coastline. The camp's well-preserved structures and interpretive exhibits shed light on the military strategies employed by the American forces and their efforts to maintain a peaceful coexistence with the British soldiers during the standoff.

Exploring American Camp offers a glimpse into the daily lives of the soldiers who inhabited the area. The barracks and officers' quarters have been meticulously restored, allowing visitors to step into the past and imagine the soldiers' routines, interactions, and challenges. The displays and artifacts within the buildings offer insights into the soldiers' equipment, provisions, and the technologies of the era.

One of the highlights of a visit to American Camp is the opportunity to hike along the picturesque trails that wind through the prairies and along the coastline. These trails not only offer stunning views of the island's natural beauty but also allow visitors to trace the footsteps of the soldiers and gain a sense of the strategic advantages that the location provided during the standoff.

As you explore the camp, take a moment to pause at the peaceful and poignant memorial to those who lost their lives during the Pig War. The memorial serves as a reminder of the importance of diplomacy and the ultimate peaceful resolution that was reached between the United States and Great Britain.

Whale Museum: Delve into the world of whales through interactive exhibits and educational displays, highlighting the region's rich marine ecosystem and the ongoing conservation efforts.

For those fascinated by the majestic creatures that inhabit the waters surrounding the San Juan Islands, a visit to the Whale Museum is an absolute must. Located in Friday Harbor on San Juan Island, this unique institution is dedicated to promoting awareness and understanding of whales, their habitat, and the importance of marine conservation.

Upon entering the museum, visitors are greeted by an array of interactive exhibits that engage the senses and provide a comprehensive overview of the world of whales. From life-size replicas and skeletons to multimedia presentations and immersive displays, the museum offers a wealth of information about various whale species, their behaviors, migration patterns, and the challenges they face in today's changing world.

One of the highlights of the Whale Museum is the sound exhibit, where visitors can listen to the hauntingly beautiful songs and calls of different whale species. This immersive experience allows guests to appreciate the unique vocalizations and communication methods employed by these remarkable creatures.

The museum also showcases the ongoing efforts of scientists, researchers, and conservationists to protect and preserve the fragile marine ecosystem of the San Juan Islands. Visitors can learn about the impact of human activities on whales and the steps being taken to mitigate these effects. Interactive displays demonstrate how individual actions can contribute to the conservation of marine life and inspire visitors to become stewards of the oceans.

In addition to the exhibits, the Whale Museum offers educational programs, lectures, and workshops for visitors of all ages. These opportunities provide a deeper understanding of marine ecology, wildlife conservation, and the interconnectedness of the ecosystem.

As you explore the museum, be sure to visit the gift shop, which offers a variety of unique and eco-friendly items, including books, artwork, clothing, and souvenirs. By supporting the Whale Museum, visitors contribute to the ongoing research, education, and conservation efforts that are vital for the protection of whales and their habitat.

Whether you're a marine enthusiast, an animal lover, or simply curious about the wonders of the sea, a visit to the Whale Museum promises an enlightening and enriching experience that highlights the importance of preserving our oceans and the incredible creatures that call them home.

Here are a few more historic sites and cultural attractions on San Juan Island:

Roche Harbor Historic Village: Located on the northwest side of the island, Roche Harbor is a charming historic village that showcases the island's rich history and maritime heritage. Explore the beautifully preserved buildings, including the Hotel de Haro and the Roche Harbor Lime and Cement Company office. Visit the McMillin Mausoleum, a stunning architectural gem, and learn about the town's intriguing past through informative plaques and exhibits.

San Juan Historical Museum: Situated in Friday Harbor, the San Juan Historical Museum provides a fascinating glimpse into the island's past. Housed in a former dairy barn, the museum features exhibits and artifacts that highlight the island's Native American history, early European settlement, and maritime traditions. Discover the stories of the island's pioneers, browse through photographs and memorabilia, and gain a deeper appreciation for the island's cultural heritage.

Pelindaba Lavender Farm: Immerse yourself in the sights and scents of lavender at Pelindaba Lavender Farm, located in the heart of San Juan Island. Stroll through fields of vibrant purple blooms and learn about the cultivation and uses of lavender through guided tours. Browse the on-site store, which offers an array of lavender-infused products, from essential oils and soaps to culinary treats and skincare items.

Westcott Bay Sculpture Park: Art enthusiasts should not miss a visit to Westcott Bay Sculpture Park, a hidden gem nestled on the western side of San Juan Island. This unique outdoor gallery features an ever-changing collection of sculptures created by local and international artists. Explore the park's winding paths and wooded areas as you encounter captivating works of art that harmoniously blend with the natural surroundings.

San Juan Islands Museum of Art (IMA): Located in Friday Harbor, the IMA is a contemporary art museum that showcases a diverse range of local and regional artwork. The museum features rotating exhibitions of paintings, sculptures, photography, and mixed media, providing visitors with an opportunity to engage with the vibrant arts community of the San Juan Islands. Check the museum's schedule for special events, artist talks, and workshops that further enrich the artistic experience.

Nature and Wildlife Encounters:

Lime Kiln Point State Park: Known as the Whale Watching Park, this scenic park offers excellent opportunities to spot orcas from the shore. Learn about the marine life and the park's historic lime kiln while enjoying picturesque coastal views.

Nestled on the western edge of San Juan Island, Lime Kiln Point State Park is a true gem for both nature enthusiasts and whale lovers alike. This park, often referred to as the Whale Watching Park, is renowned for its prime location to witness the majestic orcas that frequent the waters of the Salish Sea.

As visitors enter the park, they are greeted by a panoramic vista of the Strait of Juan de Fuca, with its sparkling blue waters stretching out to the horizon. The park's coastal cliffs provide an ideal vantage point for observing the graceful orcas as they navigate through the sea. From May to October, these magnificent creatures, also known as killer whales, pass by Lime Kiln Point during their seasonal migrations, making it a popular destination for avid whale watchers.

To enhance the whale-watching experience, the park features an interpretive center that offers educational exhibits and informative displays about the marine life in the area. Visitors can learn about the different species of whales that inhabit the Salish Sea, including orcas, humpback whales, and minke whales. The center also provides insights into the ongoing research and conservation efforts dedicated to protecting these extraordinary creatures and their fragile ecosystem.

While the main attraction of Lime Kiln Point State Park is undoubtedly the opportunity to witness orcas in their natural habitat, there is much more to discover within the park's boundaries. One notable feature is the historic lime kiln, which dates back to the late 19th century. The lime kiln was once used to convert limestone into quicklime, an essential component in the production of building materials. Today, the remnants of this historic structure serve as a reminder of the region's industrial past and offer a glimpse into the island's history.

As visitors stroll along the park's trails, they are treated to breathtaking coastal views, with rugged cliffs, towering trees, and vibrant wildflowers creating a picturesque backdrop. The network of trails provides opportunities for leisurely walks and hikes, allowing visitors to immerse themselves in the park's natural beauty and perhaps catch a glimpse of other wildlife, such as bald eagles, harbor seals, and seabirds.

For those seeking a closer connection to the marine environment, Lime Kiln Point State Park offers a unique experience through the Whale Bell Program. This program encourages visitors to ring a bell whenever they spot a whale from the park's shoreline. The ringing of the bell not only creates a sense of shared excitement but also serves as a citizen science initiative, contributing to ongoing research and monitoring of whale populations in the area.

San Juan Islands Sculpture Park: Wander through an outdoor art gallery featuring a diverse collection of sculptures by local and international artists. Take in the natural beauty as you appreciate the blend of art and nature.

For art enthusiasts and nature lovers, the San Juan Islands Sculpture Park provides a truly captivating experience that seamlessly blends artistic expression with the stunning natural surroundings. Located on San Juan Island, this unique outdoor gallery showcases a diverse collection of sculptures created by both local and international artists.

As visitors enter the sculpture park, they are immediately enveloped by the peaceful ambiance and the harmonious integration of art into the island's landscape. The park's trails wind through meadows, forests, and waterfront areas, allowing visitors to discover each sculpture in its own distinctive setting. The sculptures themselves encompass a wide range of styles, materials, and themes, representing the creativity and vision of the artists.

Wandering through the park, visitors are encouraged to engage with the sculptures on a personal level, examining the intricate details, contemplating their meanings, and appreciating the skill and artistry behind each piece. The outdoor setting adds an additional layer of depth to the artwork, as the changing light, seasons, and natural elements interact with the sculptures, creating an ever-evolving visual experience.

Beyond its artistic offerings, the San Juan Islands Sculpture Park also serves as a sanctuary for wildlife, providing a haven for birds, butterflies, and other creatures. As visitors explore the park, they may encounter deer peacefully grazing, squirrels scampering through the trees, or a chorus of birdsong filling the air. The combination of art and nature creates a harmonious environment where visitors can connect with both their artistic sensibilities and the natural world.

The sculpture park also hosts various events and exhibitions throughout the year, including artist talks, workshops, and interactive installations. These events provide opportunities for visitors to engage with the artists, gain insights into their creative processes, and deepen their understanding and appreciation of the sculptures.

Before leaving the sculpture park, be sure to visit the gift shop, which offers a curated selection of artwork, jewelry, and other unique items created by local artists. By supporting the San Juan Islands Sculpture Park, visitors contribute to the promotion of art in the community and the preservation of this enchanting outdoor gallery.

Whether you find inspiration in the intricate sculptures, the tranquil surroundings, or the seamless blend of art and nature, a visit to the San Juan Islands Sculpture Park is a truly enriching experience that celebrates the creativity of the human spirit while fostering a deep connection with the natural world.

Lopez Island: Experience the laid-back atmosphere, scenic biking routes, and local farms that make Lopez Island a beloved destination.

Experience the laid-back atmosphere, scenic biking routes, and local farms that make Lopez Island a beloved destination.

Biking and Outdoor Exploration:

Lopez Island Bike Routes: Discover the joy of biking on the island's well-maintained routes, passing through picturesque farmlands, charming hamlets, and breathtaking coastal scenery. Rent a bike and set off on a leisurely ride to embrace the island's relaxed pace.

Lopez Island is a cyclist's paradise, offering a network of bike routes that meander through the island's idyllic landscapes. Known for its serene atmosphere and unspoiled natural beauty, Lopez Island provides the perfect setting for a leisurely bike ride, allowing you to explore at your own pace and immerse yourself in the island's unique charm.

Renting a bike is easy on Lopez Island, with several rental shops conveniently located near the ferry terminal. Whether you prefer a classic cruiser or a sturdy mountain bike, you can find the perfect set of wheels to embark on your two-wheeled adventure. Once you've secured your bike, it's time to hit the road and experience the island's captivating scenery.

One of the most popular bike routes on Lopez Island is the Lopez Village Loop. This scenic loop takes you through the heart of the island, starting and ending in the charming village of Lopez. As you pedal along, you'll pass through rolling farmlands, where you'll be greeted by fields of vibrant wildflowers, grazing horses, and picturesque barns. Take a moment to breathe in the fragrant scent of freshly cut hay and listen to the peaceful sounds of nature that envelop you.

The Lopez Village Loop also allows you to explore the island's quaint hamlets. As you cycle through these small communities, you'll discover local businesses, cozy cafes, and artisan shops that reflect the island's creative spirit and sense of community. Don't be surprised if you find yourself stopping frequently to browse unique handmade crafts, sample delicious baked goods, or strike up conversations with friendly locals who are always eager to share stories and recommendations.

One notable stop along the Lopez Village Loop is Lopez Island Vineyards. Nestled amidst rolling vineyards and scenic vistas, this family-owned winery offers a delightful opportunity to savor locally produced wines. Take a break from your bike ride and indulge in a wine tasting experience, where you can sample a variety of wines crafted with passion and dedication. Raise a glass to the island's natural beauty and the rich agricultural heritage that defines Lopez Island.

Another highlight of biking on Lopez Island is the opportunity to soak in the island's breathtaking coastal scenery. The Lopez Island coastline boasts rugged cliffs, secluded coves, and expansive views of the Salish Sea. As you pedal along the coastal roads, you'll catch glimpses of sparkling blue waters, and if you're lucky, you might even spot a pod of orcas swimming in the distance.

One must-visit destination along the coast is Shark Reef Park, located on the southwestern tip of Lopez Island. This protected marine area offers a tranquil oasis where you can pause your bike ride and enjoy a leisurely stroll along the shoreline. As you walk along the beach, keep an eye out for harbor seals basking in the sun on nearby rocks, while seabirds gracefully glide overhead. During low tide, the intertidal zone comes alive with fascinating creatures such as starfish, anemones, and crabs. It's a perfect spot to immerse yourself in the island's natural wonders and gain a deeper appreciation for the delicate marine ecosystem.

After a rewarding day of biking and exploration, you can unwind and replenish your energy at one of Lopez Island's charming eateries. From farm-to-table restaurants to cozy cafes, the island offers a variety of culinary delights to suit every palate. Indulge in freshly caught seafood, organic produce sourced from local farms, and artisanal cheeses that showcase the island's agricultural bounty. As you savor each bite, you'll not only satisfy your taste buds but also support the island's vibrant food culture and sustainable practices.

Lopez Island's bike routes cater to all levels of cyclists, from casual riders seeking a leisurely adventure to more experienced cyclists looking for longer and more challenging rides. The island's relatively flat terrain makes it accessible for riders of all ages and fitness levels, ensuring that everyone can enjoy the beauty of Lopez Island on two wheels.

Whether you're exploring the farmlands, pedaling through charming hamlets, or soaking in the coastal vistas, biking on Lopez Island is an experience that will leave you with lasting memories. It's a chance to disconnect from the hectic pace of everyday life and reconnect with nature, the local community, and your own sense of adventure. So, rent a bike, hop on, and let the enchanting landscapes of Lopez Island unfold before you as you embrace the island's relaxed pace and discover the true joy of cycling in this Pacific Northwest gem.

Farm-to-Table Delights and Local Culture:

Lopez Village: Explore the quaint village center, where you'll find a variety of local shops, cafes, and restaurants offering delicious farm-fresh cuisine and locally made products.

Nestled on the eastern side of Lopez Island, Lopez Village is a charming hub that captures the essence of the island's laid-back atmosphere and community spirit. With its picturesque setting and welcoming ambiance, it's the perfect place to immerse yourself in the local culture and indulge in the island's culinary delights.

As you wander through Lopez Village, you'll encounter a delightful array of shops, each offering unique treasures and locally crafted goods. From boutique clothing stores to art galleries, there's something to pique everyone's interest. One popular stop is Paper Scissors on the Rock, a delightful stationery and gift shop known for its curated selection of handmade cards, journals, and local artisan creations. Whether you're looking for a special souvenir or a thoughtful gift, the village shops provide a diverse range of options to suit every taste.

Lopez Island is renowned for its agricultural heritage, and this is reflected in the village's thriving farm-to-table scene. The local cafes and restaurants in Lopez Village take pride in sourcing ingredients from the island's farms and fisheries, ensuring that each dish is bursting with freshness and flavor. Stop by Holly B's Bakery, a beloved institution known for its delectable pastries, bread, and pies made from scratch with locally sourced ingredients. Indulge in a flaky croissant, savor a slice of freshly baked berry pie, or try their famous cinnamon rolls. The bakery's cozy atmosphere and mouthwatering aromas make it the ideal spot to start your day or enjoy an afternoon treat.

For those seeking a savory dining experience, Vita's Wildly Delicious offers a farm-to-table menu that celebrates the island's bounty. Their ever-changing menu showcases the best of Lopez Island's seasonal produce, seafood, and grass-fed meats. From fresh salads featuring vibrant greens and locally foraged ingredients to hearty mains like pan-seared salmon with a citrus glaze, each dish tells a story of Lopez Island's culinary heritage.

Lopez Village also boasts a vibrant arts scene, with several galleries showcasing the work of local artists. The Chimera Gallery is a must-visit destination for art enthusiasts, featuring a diverse collection of paintings, sculptures, pottery, and jewelry created by talented island artists. Take your time exploring the gallery's curated displays, and perhaps even find a unique piece to bring home as a lasting memento of your Lopez Island experience.

To delve deeper into the island's rich history and cultural heritage, a visit to the Lopez Island Historical Society and Museum is highly recommended. Housed in a beautifully restored building, the museum offers fascinating exhibits that transport visitors back in time. Learn about the island's agricultural roots and the important role farming played in shaping the community. Discover the stories of early settlers who tilled the land, planted orchards, and established dairy farms, leaving an enduring legacy that can still be witnessed on the island today.

The museum's exhibits also shed light on Lopez Island's deep connection to the sea. Fishing has long been a way of life for the island's residents, and the museum showcases the traditions and techniques passed down through generations. From the iconic wooden fishing boats to the tools and equipment used in the industry, the exhibits provide a glimpse into the challenges and triumphs of the island's seafaring history.

Perhaps the most captivating aspect of Lopez Island's history is the unique community spirit that permeates every aspect of island life. The museum's exhibits pay homage to the tight-knit community that has thrived on the island, showcasing the stories of resilience, cooperation, and the strong bonds that tie the Lopez Island residents together. Through photographs, personal accounts, and artifacts, visitors gain a deeper understanding of the island's heritage and the enduring spirit that has made Lopez Island a cherished place to live and visit.

As you explore Lopez Village and delve into the island's past at the Lopez Island Historical Society and Museum, you'll come to appreciate the island's sense of community, its commitment to sustainability, and the rich tapestry of stories that have shaped Lopez Island into the unique destination it is today. Whether you're strolling through the village shops, savoring farm-fresh cuisine, or discovering the island's history, Lopez Village offers a warm and inviting experience that will leave a lasting impression.

Whether you're seeking outdoor adventures, historical exploration, or a relaxing getaway, Orcas Island, San Juan Island, and Lopez Island offer distinct experiences that capture the essence of the San Juan Islands.

Chapter 3: Hidden Gems and Lesser-Known Islands

Shaw Island: Uncover the peaceful and serene Shaw Island, home to a tight-knit community, picturesque hikes, and the stunning Shaw Island County Park.

Nestled between Orcas Island and Lopez Island, Shaw Island is a hidden gem that offers a tranquil retreat away from the bustling crowds. As you step off the ferry onto the island, you'll immediately sense the island's unique atmosphere, characterized by a strong sense of community and a slower pace of life. Shaw Island is a place where time seems to slow down, allowing visitors to truly unwind and connect with nature.

One of the highlights of Shaw Island is Shaw Island County Park, a pristine waterfront park that beckons visitors with its unspoiled beauty. The park stretches along the island's shoreline, offering breathtaking panoramic views of the surrounding islands and the sparkling waters of the Salish Sea. Take a leisurely stroll along the sandy beaches, feeling the cool breeze on your skin and listening to the gentle lapping of the waves. The park also features picnic areas, where you can enjoy a delightful outdoor lunch while savoring the tranquility of the surroundings. For those with a love for boating, Shaw Island County Park offers a convenient boat launch, making it an ideal starting point for exploring the surrounding waterways.

One of the joys of Shaw Island is the opportunity to immerse yourself in nature. The island boasts a network of picturesque hiking trails that wind through dense forests, meadows, and along the rugged coastline. Lace up your hiking boots and embark on the Shaw Island Loop Trail, a 7-mile loop that showcases the island's diverse landscapes. As you wander through towering trees and moss-covered trails, keep an eye out for wildlife. Shaw Island is home to a variety of wildlife species, including deer, eagles, and a wide range of bird species. Birdwatchers will be particularly delighted by the chance to spot rare migratory birds that visit the island during certain seasons.

As you explore the island, you'll encounter charming farmsteads, historic buildings, and friendly locals who embody the island's sense of community. Shaw Island has a strong agricultural heritage, and you may come across local farmers tending to their crops or raising livestock. If you're lucky, you might even have the opportunity to purchase fresh produce directly from the farms. The island's tight-knit community is evident in its historic buildings, some of which have been preserved for generations. One such gem is the Shaw Island Library, a small but cozy library housed in a historic building. Step inside and be greeted by shelves lined with a curated collection of books. Spend a peaceful afternoon immersed in the island's literary culture, finding a quiet corner to dive into a captivating story or simply enjoying the tranquility of the surroundings.

Shaw Island's sense of community extends beyond its natural and cultural attractions. The island hosts various events and gatherings throughout the year, providing opportunities for both locals and visitors to come together and celebrate. From summer concerts in the park to community potlucks, these events offer a chance to connect with the island's residents and experience the warmth and hospitality that Shaw Island is known for.

If you're looking for a place to stay on Shaw Island, you'll find a handful of accommodations that offer a peaceful and intimate experience. Cozy bed and breakfasts and vacation rentals provide comfortable and welcoming retreats, allowing you to fully immerse yourself in the island's serenity. Wake up to the sound of birdsong, sip your morning coffee while gazing at the breathtaking views, and embrace the slower pace of island life.

Whether you're seeking solitude in nature, a deeper connection with a tight-knit community, or simply a break from the fast-paced world, Shaw Island is a destination that offers all of these and more. It's a place where the beauty of the landscape is matched only by the warmth of its people, making it a truly unforgettable experience. Shaw Island is a hidden paradise waiting to be discovered, offering a sanctuary for those seeking peace, serenity, and a genuine connection with nature and community.

Sucia Island: Venture to this marine state park, where stunning sea caves, sandy beaches, and incredible marine life await your exploration.

Just a short boat ride away from the main islands lies Sucia Island, a marine state park that enchants visitors with its rugged beauty and abundant marine ecosystems. As you approach the island, you'll be greeted by towering sandstone cliffs, sculpted by the forces of wind and water over centuries.

Sucia Island's greatest allure lies beneath the surface of the water. Strap on your snorkeling gear or hop on a kayak to discover the vibrant underwater world that thrives in the park's clear, turquoise waters. Dive into a realm teeming with colorful marine life, from playful seals to schools of shimmering fish. The waters around Sucia Island are part of the Salish Sea, a nutrient-rich marine ecosystem that supports a diverse array of species. Keep an eye out for the elusive and graceful orcas that occasionally pass by the island, their dorsal fins breaking the surface in a majestic display. As you explore the underwater landscape, you may also encounter sea stars, anemones, and crabs, adding bursts of color to the rocky seabed.

One of the most captivating features of Sucia Island is the presence of sea caves that have been carved into the island's cliffs by the relentless pounding of the waves. These sea caves are a natural wonder, beckoning adventurers to explore their mysterious depths. Kayakers can navigate through the narrow passages, feeling the cool spray of seawater and marveling at the intricate rock formations illuminated by the beams of sunlight that filter through openings in the caves. It's a truly otherworldly experience, as you find yourself in a hidden realm shaped by the relentless power of the ocean.

Above the waterline, Sucia Island boasts several sandy beaches, perfect for sunbathing, picnicking, or beachcombing. With names like Shallow Bay, Ewing Cove, and Fox Cove, each beach offers its own unique characteristics and scenic views. Shallow Bay, as the name suggests, features a gently sloping shoreline that allows visitors to wade into the water and explore the tide pools teeming with marine life. Ewing Cove offers a more secluded and tranquil setting, where you can unwind and listen to the soothing sound of waves lapping against the shore. Fox Cove, with its expansive sandy beach, invites visitors to take long walks, bask in the sun, or build sandcastles with their loved ones. Whether you're seeking solitude or a place to enjoy family fun, Sucia Island's beaches provide the perfect backdrop for a memorable day at the seashore.

To fully immerse yourself in the natural wonders of Sucia Island, consider camping overnight. The park offers primitive campsites equipped with picnic tables, fire pits, and composting toilets. Fall asleep under a canopy of stars and wake up to the soothing sounds of waves crashing against the shore, immersing yourself in the island's untamed beauty. Camping on Sucia Island allows you to experience the island's tranquility after the day-trippers have left, offering a unique opportunity to connect with nature and disconnect from the distractions of modern life.

As you explore Sucia Island, keep an eye out for the island's rich birdlife. The park is home to a variety of bird species, including bald eagles, ospreys, herons, and cormorants. Watch as they soar through the sky, gracefully diving into the water to catch their prey or perching on rocky outcrops, surveying their surroundings. Sucia Island is a birdwatcher's paradise, offering opportunities to observe these magnificent creatures in their natural habitat.

It's worth noting that Sucia Island's popularity has led to restrictions on the number of boats and visitors allowed on the island at any given time. This ensures the preservation of its fragile ecosystems and allows visitors to fully appreciate the unspoiled beauty of the park. It's advisable to plan your visit in advance and obtain any necessary permits or reservations to ensure a seamless and enjoyable experience.

Sucia Island is a true gem within the San Juan archipelago, offering a captivating blend of natural wonders both above and below the waterline. From the enchanting sea caves to the serene sandy beaches, every corner of this marine state park invites exploration and wonder. Whether you choose to snorkel amidst colorful marine life, paddle through hidden sea caves, or simply relax on the shores and soak in the island's untamed beauty, Sucia Island promises an unforgettable experience for all who venture there.

Blakely Island: Discover the exclusive and private island, offering secluded beaches, waterfront estates, and unparalleled natural beauty.

Blakely Island, with its exclusivity and privacy, has long been a well-kept secret among those seeking an escape from the demands of modern life. As you venture onto the island, you'll immediately feel the sense of tranquility that pervades the air. The absence of crowds and the limited number of visitors contribute to the island's serene atmosphere, allowing you to fully immerse yourself in the natural wonders that abound.

The beaches of Blakely Island are truly gems of solitude. Picture yourself walking barefoot along the sandy shoreline, with only the sound of seagulls and gentle waves breaking the silence. The absence of noise pollution and the absence of development along the coast contribute to the unspoiled beauty of the island's beaches. Find a comfortable spot on the sand, unfold your beach chair, and allow the stresses of everyday life to melt away as you bask in the warm sun and admire the pristine surroundings.

One of the most renowned beaches on Blakely Island is Pebble Beach. As its name suggests, this beach is adorned with smooth, polished pebbles, brought in by the tides and shaped by the elements over time. The beach is a testament to the natural forces at play, offering a captivating sight and a perfect place to collect unique stones as souvenirs of your time on the island.

For those with a sense of adventure, Blakely Island's trails beckon to be explored. Lace up your hiking boots and set off on the island's pathways, which wind through lush old-growth forests. As you walk amidst towering trees, you'll feel a deep connection to nature and a sense of peace that can only be found in such pristine surroundings. Keep your eyes peeled for the island's wildlife inhabitants - from graceful deer that gracefully roam the forest to mischievous foxes darting through the undergrowth. Blakely Island is also a haven for bird enthusiasts, with a variety of species flitting about, their vibrant colors contrasting with the verdant foliage.

One particularly enchanting trail on Blakely Island is the Hidden Valley Trail. This moderate-level hike takes you through a hidden valley, where sunlight filters through the canopy above, creating an ethereal glow. The trail leads to a stunning viewpoint, where you can witness panoramic vistas of the Salish Sea and the neighboring islands. It's the perfect spot to pause, take a deep breath, and appreciate the sheer beauty of the natural world.

Blakely Island's allure extends beyond its terrestrial wonders to the surrounding waters. The island is a gateway to captivating marine life and unforgettable aquatic experiences. Rent a kayak or paddleboard and set out on an exploration of the island's coast, gliding over crystal-clear waters. Along the way, keep an eye out for harbor seals basking on rocky outcroppings, their curious eyes following your every move. If you're lucky, you might spot playful otters frolicking in the kelp beds or catch a glimpse of a majestic orca breaching in the distance.

As the day draws to a close, indulge in the island's luxurious offerings. Blakely Island is home to an exclusive community of waterfront estates and vacation rentals, providing an unparalleled level of comfort and seclusion. These properties boast breathtaking views of the Salish Sea and the surrounding islands, offering a front-row seat to the ever-changing hues of the sky during sunset. Imagine sipping a glass of local wine on a private deck, the soft breeze caressing your skin as you watch the sun dip below the horizon, painting the sky in a vibrant palette of oranges, pinks, and purples. It's a truly magical experience that will leave an indelible mark on your memory.

Blakely Island is a place where time seems to slow down, allowing you to reconnect with nature and find solace in its unspoiled beauty. The exclusivity and seclusion of the island create an intimate atmosphere that lends itself to relaxation, reflection, and rejuvenation. Whether you spend your days lounging on the secluded beaches, hiking through enchanting forests, or exploring the marine wonders, Blakely Island offers an unparalleled escape from the outside world, leaving you with a sense of serenity that will stay with you long after you leave its shores.

Note: Access to Blakely Island is limited to property owners and their guests. Public access is restricted, and permission is required to visit the island.

Chapter 4: Outdoor Adventures

San Juan Islands offer a plethora of outdoor adventures for nature enthusiasts and thrill-seekers alike. In this chapter, we will explore the exciting activities that await you in the archipelago's pristine natural surroundings.

Kayaking and Boating: Embark on an aquatic adventure, exploring the diverse waterways and wildlife-rich habitats around the islands.

Embark on an aquatic adventure and discover the beauty of the San Juan Islands from the water. Whether you're an experienced kayaker or a novice paddler, the calm and protected waterways provide the perfect setting for exploration. The archipelago's unique geography, with its intricate channels, sheltered coves, and hidden bays, offers endless possibilities for unforgettable kayak journeys.

Renting a kayak is a popular option for those looking to explore at their own pace. Local outfitters provide well-maintained kayaks and all the necessary gear, ensuring a safe and enjoyable experience. Before setting off, take a moment to familiarize yourself with the basics of kayaking and safety procedures. The friendly staff at the rental shops are always happy to provide guidance and recommendations based on your skill level and interests.

If you prefer a more immersive and educational experience, joining a guided kayak tour is an excellent choice. Knowledgeable guides will lead you through the island's waterways, sharing fascinating insights about the local ecosystem, wildlife, and history. They know the best routes to take, ensuring you don't miss any of the hidden gems along the way. Some tours even offer the opportunity to learn about the traditional practices of the Coast Salish people, who have lived in harmony with the islands' environment for centuries.

As you paddle along, you'll be surrounded by the breathtaking coastal landscapes that define the San Juan Islands. Towering cliffs, rocky shorelines, and emerald-green forests provide a stunning backdrop as you glide through the water. The islands' tranquil atmosphere creates a sense of serenity and allows you to connect with nature on a deeper level. Listen to the soothing sounds of the water lapping against your kayak, the calls of seabirds echoing in the distance, and the gentle rustling of leaves as you pass by secluded beaches.

Keep your eyes peeled for the curious harbor seals that frequently pop their heads above the water, observing your journey with playful eyes. These charismatic creatures often swim alongside kayakers, seemingly intrigued by their human companions. You may also spot adorable otters floating on their backs, cracking open shells or grooming their luxurious fur. Their playful antics never fail to bring smiles to the faces of those lucky enough to witness them.

However, the true stars of the show in the San Juan Islands are undoubtedly the orcas, also known as killer whales. These majestic creatures are a symbol of the region and draw visitors from all over the world. The waters surrounding the islands are home to three resident pods of orcas: J, K, and L pods. Each pod has its distinct family structure, vocal dialect, and hunting techniques.

Spotting an orca breaching the surface is a sight that leaves a lasting impression. As you paddle through the Salish Sea, you might suddenly hear the distinctive sound of a blow, followed by the sight of a massive dorsal fin slicing through the water. These awe-inspiring creatures move gracefully, their sleek black and white bodies contrasting against the blue hues of the ocean. It's a moment that fills you with a sense of wonder and appreciation for the natural world.

While orca sightings are never guaranteed, the San Juan Islands offer some of the best opportunities in the world to observe these magnificent creatures in their natural habitat. Kayaking provides a unique advantage, allowing you to navigate quietly and closely observe their behavior without disturbing them. However, it's crucial to maintain a respectful distance and follow guidelines to ensure the safety and well-being of the orcas and other marine wildlife.

Boating enthusiasts will also find plenty of opportunities to set sail and navigate the surrounding waters of the San Juan Islands. Renting a sailboat or joining a chartered boat tour opens up new horizons and allows you to venture further into the archipelago. The islands' pristine marine environment is a haven for wildlife, and you'll likely encounter a diverse array of seabirds, porpoises, and other marine creatures during your boating adventures.

As you sail from island to island, you'll have the chance to explore hidden coves and anchor in secluded spots. Drop anchor in a calm bay and dive into the crystal-clear waters for a refreshing swim, or simply relax on deck and soak in the tranquil ambiance of your surroundings. Keep your camera ready, as unexpected wildlife encounters are not uncommon in these waters.

Seabirds, such as majestic bald eagles, soar overhead, their keen eyes scanning the water for potential prey. These iconic birds of prey are a common sight in the San Juan Islands, and witnessing their aerial acrobatics is a treat for birdwatchers and nature enthusiasts. Keep an eye out for their massive nests perched high atop the trees along the shoreline.

The archipelago's marine environment is also home to a variety of porpoises, including the harbor porpoise and Dall's porpoise. These small, playful cetaceans can often be seen darting through the waves, their sleek bodies effortlessly cutting through the water. If you're lucky, you might even spot a humpback whale breaching in the distance, its enormous body launching itself out of the water before crashing back with a mighty splash.

Whichever aquatic adventure you choose in the San Juan Islands, be it kayaking or boating, you'll be rewarded with unforgettable experiences and a profound connection with the natural wonders that surround you. These activities offer a unique perspective, allowing you to immerse yourself in the archipelago's pristine marine environment and create memories that will last a lifetime. So, grab a paddle or set sail, and let the beauty of the San Juan Islands unfold before your eyes.

Hiking and Nature Trails: Lace up your boots and traverse the scenic trails, taking you through old-growth forests, coastal bluffs, and panoramic viewpoints.

Strap on your hiking boots and immerse yourself in the natural wonders of the San Juan Islands. With a network of well-maintained trails catering to all skill levels, these islands offer a diverse range of hiking experiences that will leave you in awe of the breathtaking vistas and encounters with the region's flora and fauna.

One of the standout hiking destinations in the San Juan Islands is Mount Constitution on Orcas Island. Located within Moran State Park, this moderate hike takes you through mossy forests, providing a cool and refreshing ambiance as you ascend to the summit. The trail is well-marked, and as you make your way up, you'll be surrounded by towering trees and the sound of birdsong. Take a moment to appreciate the tranquility and serenity of the forest, feeling a connection with nature that is unique to this beautiful archipelago.

Upon reaching the summit of Mount Constitution, a spectacular panoramic view awaits. Gaze out over the surrounding islands, their lush greenery contrasting against the sparkling blue waters of the Salish Sea. On a clear day, you'll even catch a glimpse of the distant snow-capped peaks of the Cascade Range. It's a breathtaking sight that reminds you of the grandeur and vastness of the natural world. Take a seat on the stone observation tower and soak in the beauty that stretches out before you, knowing that this moment is one you'll cherish forever.

For those seeking a more leisurely stroll through ancient forests, Lime Kiln State Park on San Juan Island is a must-visit destination. As you wander along the tranquil trails, the scent of moss and damp earth fills the air, creating a sensory experience that transports you to another realm. The dense forests envelop you in a sense of calm and wonder, with towering trees that have stood for centuries. Listen to the rustle of leaves underfoot, feeling a connection with the history and resilience of these old-growth forests.

One of the highlights of Lime Kiln State Park is the historic lime kiln itself. As you approach the kiln, you'll learn about its fascinating past and its role in the island's history. This piece of industrial heritage stands as a testament to the human impact on the landscape, a reminder that the San Juan Islands have long been shaped by the hands of those who came before us.

Continuing along the trails, you'll eventually find yourself at the rugged shoreline. This is a prime spot for wildlife encounters, as the resident orca population often passes by these waters. Keep a watchful eye on the horizon, and if you're lucky, you may witness these majestic creatures gracefully gliding through the waves. The sight of an orca breaching or the sound of their distinctive blows is something that will stay with you forever, a cherished memory of your time in the San Juan Islands.

While exploring the trails of the San Juan Islands, you'll encounter an incredible diversity of flora and fauna. The islands are home to a wide range of plant species, from towering firs and cedars to delicate wildflowers that paint the landscape with vibrant colors. Keep your eyes peeled for glimpses of deer, squirrels, and other woodland creatures as they traverse their natural habitat.

As you hike, don't forget to look up to the sky, for the San Juan Islands are a birdwatcher's paradise. The islands' diverse ecosystems attract a wide array of avian species. Bald eagles, with their majestic wingspans, can often be spotted soaring overhead, their white heads and dark bodies standing out against the backdrop of the blue sky. The calls of songbirds fill the air, adding a melodious soundtrack to your hiking adventures.

To enhance your hiking experience in the San Juan Islands, it's essential to come prepared. Wear comfortable hiking shoes and dress in layers, as the weather can change throughout the day. Carry a backpack with essentials such as water, snacks, a map, and a camera to capture the stunning views and wildlife encounters you may come across.

Remember to practice Leave No Trace principles during your hikes, respecting the fragile ecosystem and minimizing your impact on the environment. Stay on designated trails, refrain from picking or disturbing plants and wildlife, and pack out any trash you may have. By being a responsible hiker, you contribute to the preservation of these beautiful natural spaces for future generations to enjoy.

So, whether you choose to ascend to the summit of Mount Constitution on Orcas Island for awe-inspiring coastal views or take a leisurely stroll through the old-growth forests of Lime Kiln State Park on San Juan Island, the hiking experiences in the San Juan Islands are sure to leave you with a profound appreciation for the region's natural wonders. These trails offer a chance to disconnect from the hustle and bustle of daily life and reconnect with the awe-inspiring beauty of the natural world. So lace up your boots, breathe in the crisp island air, and let the trails of the San Juan Islands guide you to unforgettable adventures and unforgettable memories.

Whale Watching and Wildlife Encounters: Learn about the best spots to witness majestic orcas, seals, bald eagles, and other fascinating creatures.

The San Juan Islands are renowned worldwide for their exceptional whale-watching opportunities. This archipelago is blessed with abundant marine life, including the iconic orcas, which are the main attraction for visitors seeking a close encounter with these magnificent creatures.

Embarking on a guided whale-watching tour in the San Juan Islands is a truly awe-inspiring experience. Local operators offer expert knowledge and adhere to responsible wildlife viewing practices, ensuring minimal disturbance to the animals and their natural habitat. These tours provide an educational and thrilling adventure, as knowledgeable guides share fascinating insights into the behavior, ecology, and conservation efforts surrounding the orcas.

As you set out on your whale-watching excursion, the anticipation builds. The turquoise waters of the Salish Sea shimmer under the sun, reflecting the beauty of the surrounding islands. The air is filled with excitement and a sense of wonder, knowing that you are about to witness one of nature's most incredible spectacles.

As you venture further into the San Juan Islands' waters, keep a watchful eye on the horizon. Suddenly, a plume of mist breaks the surface, and the sight of a dorsal fin emerges from the water. It's the unmistakable sign that orcas are nearby. The boat slows down, allowing everyone on board to fully immerse themselves in this extraordinary encounter.

The orcas, also known as killer whales, gracefully glide through the water, their sleek black bodies contrasting against the sparkling sea. These highly intelligent and social creatures move in tight-knit family groups known as pods. The resident orca population in the San Juan Islands consists of three pods: J, K, and L pods, each with their own distinctive markings and vocal dialects.

As you observe these majestic beings in their natural habitat, you may witness their playful behaviors. Orcas breach, leaping out of the water and crashing back down with a resounding splash. They tail slap, forcefully slapping their tails against the surface, creating a dramatic display. It's a mesmerizing sight, leaving you in awe of their power and grace.

While orcas are the stars of the show, the waters surrounding the San Juan Islands are teeming with other fascinating marine life. Playful seals can often be seen basking on rocky shores or curiously swimming alongside your boat. Keep your eyes peeled for harbor porpoises darting through the waves, their sleek bodies effortlessly navigating the currents. And if you're lucky, you may even catch a glimpse of a majestic humpback whale gracefully arching its back before disappearing beneath the surface, leaving behind a trail of mist.

Above the water, the San Juan Islands are a haven for birdwatchers. Look up, and you'll often spot bald eagles soaring overhead. Their distinctive white heads and powerful wingspan make them easy to identify. These magnificent birds of prey are a symbol of the region's natural beauty and are frequently seen perched on treetops or soaring high in the sky, surveying the landscape for their next meal.

The San Juan Islands' diverse ecosystems attract a wide range of bird species, making it a paradise for avian enthusiasts. From the elegant great blue heron patiently stalking its prey along the shoreline to the colorful plumage of the tufted puffin, there is always something captivating to observe. Keep an eye out for the black oystercatcher, a charismatic shorebird with its striking black plumage and bright orange bill. The islands also provide vital nesting grounds for seabirds like the rhinoceros auklet and the pigeon guillemot.

During your birdwatching adventures, you might come across the marbled murrelet, a small seabird known for its unique nesting habits. These birds travel great distances from the ocean to inland forests, where they nest in the mossy branches of ancient trees. Witnessing the sight of a marbled murrelet flying through the dense forest canopy is a testament to the delicate balance between land and sea that exists in the San Juan Islands.

Whether you are captivated by the graceful dance of orcas, the playful antics of seals, or the regal presence of bald eagles, the San Juan Islands offer an unparalleled opportunity to connect with the natural world. As you witness these extraordinary creatures in their pristine habitat, you'll gain a deeper appreciation for the importance of conservation efforts and the delicate ecosystem that supports the rich biodiversity of the archipelago.

Remember, when venturing out to witness these natural wonders, it is crucial to prioritize responsible wildlife viewing practices. Keep a safe distance from the animals, refrain from feeding or disturbing them, and follow the guidance of your knowledgeable guides. By embracing these principles, we can ensure the protection and preservation of this remarkable ecosystem for generations to come.

Embarking on these outdoor adventures in the San Juan Islands will leave you with lasting memories of breathtaking landscapes, thrilling encounters with wildlife, and a profound appreciation for the region's natural wonders. Remember to respect the fragile ecosystem and follow guidelines to ensure the preservation of this pristine paradise for future generations.

Chapter 5: Cultural and Historical Highlights

Art and Galleries: Immerse yourself in the vibrant local arts scene, visiting galleries, studios, and art events that showcase the talent of the islands.

The San Juan Islands boast a thriving arts scene, and this chapter invites you to immerse yourself in the vibrant local culture. Whether you're an art enthusiast or simply appreciate creative expressions, the islands offer a diverse range of galleries, studios, and art events that showcase the immense talent of the region.

One of the best places to start your artistic exploration is in Friday Harbor, the largest town on San Juan Island. As you stroll through the charming streets, you'll come across numerous galleries displaying an array of artworks. From contemporary paintings to traditional sculptures, each gallery offers a unique perspective and a chance to connect with the local art community. The vibrant colors and intricate details of the artworks often reflect the awe-inspiring natural beauty that surrounds the islands.

One notable gallery in Friday Harbor is the Island Studios Art Gallery, where you can find a collective of local artists working in various mediums. Step inside the gallery, and you'll be greeted by a diverse selection of paintings, ceramics, glasswork, and jewelry. Engage with the artists themselves, who are often present to discuss their work and share their creative processes. This interaction provides a rare opportunity to gain insights into the inspiration behind their art and the techniques they employ.

Venturing beyond Friday Harbor, the smaller communities scattered across the San Juan Islands hold hidden gems of their own. In the village of Eastsound on Orcas Island, you'll discover quaint galleries tucked away in charming buildings. The Orcas Island Artworks is a cooperative gallery that showcases the works of over 50 local artists. The gallery's rustic charm and warm atmosphere create an inviting space to appreciate a wide range of artistic styles and mediums. From landscape paintings that capture the islands' breathtaking vistas to handcrafted pottery inspired by the natural elements, each piece tells a story and reflects the unique character of the San Juan Islands.

As you explore the islands, keep an eye out for special art events and festivals that celebrate the local talent. The San Juan Islands Artists' Studio Tour is a highly anticipated annual event, providing a rare opportunity to visit the working studios of renowned artists. During the tour, you can witness the creative process firsthand, interact with the artists, and gain a deeper understanding of their artistic visions. It's a chance to go beyond the gallery walls and experience the intimate spaces where masterpieces are born.

The artists of the San Juan Islands draw inspiration from the stunning landscapes, diverse wildlife, and the sense of tranquility that permeates the archipelago. Their works often reflect the interplay between humans and nature, capturing the harmony and interconnectedness that define life on the islands. Paintings may showcase the vibrant colors of wildflowers blanketing a meadow or the ethereal hues of a sunset over the glistening waters. Sculptures might depict marine creatures, paying homage to the rich biodiversity found in the surrounding seas.

While visual arts take center stage, the artistic offerings extend beyond paintings and sculptures. The islands are also home to skilled artisans who excel in creating intricate jewelry, pottery, and textiles. Inspired by their surroundings, these artisans infuse their creations with a touch of island spirit. Delicate seashells may adorn a handcrafted necklace, or the patterns on a handwoven tapestry might mirror the undulating waves of the Salish Sea. These unique pieces serve as tangible reminders of the beauty and tranquility of the San Juan Islands.

To fully immerse yourself in the local arts scene, consider participating in workshops or classes offered by resident artists. These hands-on experiences provide an opportunity to learn new techniques and unleash your own creativity. Whether it's a pottery class where you can mold clay into unique vessels or a painting workshop where you can learn to capture the essence of the islands on canvas, these enriching experiences will deepen your connection to the artistic soul of the San Juan Islands.

Art and creativity are not confined to traditional gallery spaces in the San Juan Islands. The islands themselves serve as a canvas for larger-than-life artistic expressions. Throughout the archipelago, you'll come across captivating public art installations that add an extra touch of wonder to your explorations. From vibrant murals that adorn buildings to sculptures nestled along coastal paths, these outdoor artworks seamlessly blend with the natural surroundings, creating a harmonious fusion of creativity and nature.

In the San Juan Islands, art is not just an aesthetic pursuit but an integral part of the community's identity. The local artists and artisans are passionate individuals who contribute to the cultural fabric of the islands. Their works inspire conversations, spark imagination, and foster a deeper appreciation for the beauty that surrounds us. By engaging with the local arts scene, you not only support the artists but also embark on a journey of self-discovery and creative enlightenment.

So, as you traverse the San Juan Islands, take the time to indulge your senses, explore the galleries and studios, and let the artistry of the islands wash over you. Let the strokes of a paintbrush or the intricate details of a sculpture transport you to a world where creativity knows no bounds. Whether you leave with a treasured piece of artwork or simply carry the memories of the artistic encounters, your journey through the San Juan Islands will be forever enriched by the vibrant and inspiring local arts scene.

Native American Heritage: Explore the rich history and culture of the Coast Salish people, whose presence in the San Juans dates back thousands of years.

The San Juan Islands hold a profound Native American heritage that stretches back thousands of years. The original inhabitants of the region were the Coast Salish people, who developed a deep connection with the land, sea, and wildlife. By exploring this chapter, you will gain a deeper understanding of their rich culture, traditions, and their enduring bond with the natural environment.

To fully appreciate the Native American heritage of the San Juan Islands, a visit to the Whale Museum in Friday Harbor is a must. The museum not only serves as a hub for education and research on marine mammals but also provides insights into the cultural significance of orcas to the Coast Salish people. Learn about their belief in the orcas as their relatives and the guardians of their communities. Discover the ancient stories and legends that have been passed down through generations, depicting the close connection between humans and these majestic creatures.

Engaging with local tribal members is an invaluable way to gain a firsthand understanding of their history, stories, and art. Several tribes, including the Lummi Nation and the Samish Indian Nation, have ancestral ties to the San Juan Islands. Seek out opportunities to participate in cultural events and gatherings where you can interact with tribal members, listen to their stories, and witness traditional dances and ceremonies.

As you delve deeper into the Native American heritage of the San Juan Islands, you will come across beautifully crafted art that often reflects the profound connection between humans and nature. Traditional Coast Salish art is characterized by intricate carvings, weavings, and paintings that depict wildlife, natural landscapes, and spiritual symbols. Look for local galleries and studios that showcase these works of art, allowing you to appreciate the skill and creativity of the Coast Salish artists.

Throughout the islands, you'll find archaeological sites that serve as a testament to the enduring presence of the Coast Salish people. These sites offer a glimpse into their ancient way of life and the tools they used for hunting, fishing, and gathering. Explore the shell middens, which are mounds of discarded seashells, found along the coastlines. These remnants provide evidence of the Coast Salish people's sustainable use of marine resources for sustenance and cultural practices.

The Coast Salish people have long recognized the importance of sustainable living and maintaining a harmonious relationship with the environment. Their traditional ecological knowledge and stewardship practices have been passed down through generations, reflecting a profound understanding of the interconnectedness of all living beings. As you immerse yourself in their ancestral lands, take the opportunity to learn about their sustainable practices and their efforts to protect and preserve the natural beauty of the islands.

To deepen your connection with the Native American heritage of the San Juan Islands, consider participating in cultural workshops and guided tours led by tribal members. These experiences may include storytelling sessions, traditional food tasting, and hands-on activities like basket weaving or carving. By actively engaging in these cultural experiences, you will gain a deeper appreciation for the timeless wisdom and resilience of the Coast Salish people.

As you explore the San Juan Islands, you may encounter place names that have deep cultural significance to the Coast Salish people. For instance, Shaw Island, one of the smaller islands in the archipelago, takes its name from the Shawsh-ithl, which means "skunk place" in the local language. These place names offer a glimpse into the indigenous knowledge and the intimate relationship between the people and their surroundings.

In addition to engaging with the Native American heritage, it is important to respect the customs and protocols of the

Coast Salish people. This includes seeking permission when visiting sacred sites, practicing responsible tourism, and refraining from appropriating their cultural symbols or practices. By approaching their culture with humility and respect, you can contribute to the preservation and celebration of their rich heritage.

Lighthouses and Historical Sites: Delve into the maritime heritage of the islands, visiting historic lighthouses, museums, and preserved landmarks.

The San Juan Islands have a captivating maritime history, and this section invites you to delve into the intriguing tales of lighthouses, museums, and preserved landmarks. Discover the vital role that lighthouses played in guiding ships through the treacherous waters of the archipelago.

One of the most iconic lighthouses in the San Juan Islands is the Lime Kiln Lighthouse, located on the southwestern tip of San Juan Island. It is often referred to as the "Whale Watch Park" due to its prime location for observing orcas and other marine life. As you approach the lighthouse, you'll be greeted by the picturesque coastline and breathtaking views of Haro Strait. The Lime Kiln Lighthouse, built in 1914, stands tall as a testament to the maritime heritage of the islands. Take a guided tour and learn about the fascinating history of lighthouse keeping and the crucial role this lighthouse played in ensuring the safety of ships navigating these treacherous waters.

While exploring the Lime Kiln Lighthouse, don't forget to visit the observation deck, where you can witness the beauty of the Salish Sea and spot orcas, porpoises, and seals. It's a unique opportunity to experience the intersection of nature and history, as the lighthouse continues to guide vessels while providing visitors with unforgettable wildlife encounters.

In addition to lighthouses, the San Juan Islands are home to museums that offer a glimpse into the region's rich maritime heritage. The San Juan Historical Museum, located in Friday Harbor, provides an immersive experience that takes you back in time to the days of early settlement. Explore the museum's exhibits, which include artifacts, photographs, and interactive displays that showcase the lives of the island's pioneers. Gain insights into the challenges they faced, their resourcefulness, and the industries that shaped the islands, such as fishing, logging, and agriculture. The museum also houses historic buildings, including a farmhouse and a schoolhouse, which have been carefully preserved to reflect the island's past.

Another notable historical site is the English Camp on San Juan Island, which offers a fascinating glimpse into the contentious history between the United States and Great Britain. Step back in time to 1859 when the island was occupied by both British and American forces during the Pig War dispute. Explore the preserved barracks, officers' quarters, and the formal garden that transport you to the era when tensions ran high in this remote corner of the world. Engage with knowledgeable park rangers who can share stories and anecdotes about the interactions between the soldiers and the island's native inhabitants during this peaceful standoff.

For a different perspective on history, venture to Roche Harbor on San Juan Island, a historic village that was once a booming lime and cement production center. The remnants of the lime kilns, quarries, and other industrial structures stand as silent witnesses to the island's industrial past. Take a stroll through the village's well-preserved historic district, where you can admire elegant Victorian-era buildings, including the Hotel de Haro and the Roche Harbor Chapel. The hotel, built in 1886, exudes old-world charm and offers a glimpse into the luxurious lifestyle of the island's elite during that era. The Roche Harbor Chapel, with its stunning stained glass windows and peaceful surroundings, is a testament to the community's enduring spirit.

As you explore these historical sites, you'll gain a newfound appreciation for the resilience of those who have navigated these waters throughout the centuries. The lighthouses, museums, and preserved landmarks serve as windows into the past, allowing us to glimpse the challenges, triumphs, and unique stories of the people who shaped the San Juan Islands. Whether you're a history enthusiast or simply curious about the cultural heritage of the region, immersing yourself in the maritime history of the San Juan Islands is a journey that will enrich your understanding of this captivating archipelago.

Chapter 6: Dining, Shopping, and Accommodations

Culinary Delights: Indulge in farm-to-table cuisine, seafood delicacies, and local specialties at the island's diverse restaurants and eateries.

The San Juan Islands are a paradise for food lovers, offering a culinary scene that celebrates the abundance of fresh, local ingredients. Nestled in the pristine waters of the Pacific Northwest, these islands provide a fertile ground for a vibrant food culture that showcases the region's natural bounty. From farm-to-table restaurants to cozy cafes, there is something to satisfy every palate, making the San Juan Islands a must-visit destination for those seeking a memorable dining experience.

Seafood takes center stage in the islands' culinary offerings. With the waters teeming with marine life, it's no surprise that the San Juan Islands are renowned for their mouthwatering seafood delicacies. Feast on the succulent meat of the Dungeness crab, a local treasure known for its sweet flavor and tender texture. Indulge in the Pacific Northwest salmon, which has a rich, buttery taste that melts in your mouth. The islands' pristine waters also provide the perfect conditions for cultivating oysters, resulting in plump and briny bivalves that are a delight to savor. Oyster lovers can explore various oyster bars and restaurants, where they can enjoy these delicacies freshly harvested from nearby oyster farms.

One of the highlights of dining in the San Juan Islands is the farm-to-fork movement. Local establishments prioritize sourcing their ingredients from nearby farms, showcasing the best of the islands' agricultural bounty. This commitment to using fresh, locally sourced produce ensures that diners can experience the vibrant flavors of the region while supporting sustainable farming practices. As you sit down to enjoy a meal, you can rest assured that the ingredients on your plate have been grown with care and delivered straight from the farm to your fork.

Artisanal cheese production is another thriving aspect of the islands' culinary scene. Visit local creameries and taste a variety of handcrafted cheeses made from the milk of grass-fed cows and goats. From creamy brie to tangy chèvre, the San Juan Islands offer a diverse range of artisanal cheeses that reflect the skill and dedication of local cheesemakers. Pair these delectable cheeses with locally produced wines, which benefit from the region's cool climate and unique terroir. Many wineries on the islands offer tastings and tours, providing an opportunity to savor award-winning wines while enjoying breathtaking vineyard views.

Craft beer enthusiasts will also find plenty to delight their taste buds in the San Juan Islands. The region boasts a growing craft beer scene, with local breweries producing a wide range of styles and flavors. Whether you prefer hoppy IPAs, rich stouts, or refreshing ales, you'll find a beer that suits your preferences. Head to one of the island's breweries, where you can sample small-batch brews and learn about the brewing process from the passionate brewers themselves.

No culinary journey in the San Juan Islands is complete without indulging in the sweet pleasures of handcrafted chocolates. Artisan chocolatiers on the islands create delectable treats using high-quality chocolate and locally sourced ingredients. From truffles infused with lavender harvested from nearby farms to sea salt caramels that capture the essence of the surrounding ocean, these chocolates are a testament to the islands' dedication to creating exceptional gastronomic experiences.

Whether you're seeking a fine dining experience or a casual meal with a waterfront view, the San Juan Islands offer a range of options to suit your preferences. Explore the charming towns and villages, where you'll find restaurants tucked away in historic buildings, offering intimate and cozy settings. Many of these establishments boast creative menus that change with the seasons, ensuring that diners can enjoy dishes featuring the freshest local ingredients. Sit down to a romantic dinner for two, savoring each bite as you take in the panoramic views of the islands' picturesque landscapes.

For a more casual dining experience, head to one of the islands' cafes or bistros, where you can enjoy delicious meals made with locally sourced ingredients in a relaxed atmosphere. These establishments often prioritize sustainability and community engagement, creating a welcoming space for locals and visitors alike.

In addition to its culinary delights, the San Juan Islands offer unique shopping experiences that add to the overall charm of the destination. Explore the charming boutiques and specialty shops scattered across the islands, where you can find one-of-a-kind souvenirs and handmade goods. Discover intricately designed jewelry made with locally sourced gemstones, showcasing the creativity and skill of local artisans. Peruse the shelves of pottery studios, where you can find beautifully crafted ceramics that reflect the natural beauty of the islands. Textile enthusiasts will be delighted by the selection of handwoven fabrics, showcasing the rich tapestry of the region's artistic heritage.

Art galleries in the San Juan Islands showcase a diverse range of artworks, providing an opportunity to immerse yourself in the local arts scene. From paintings and sculptures to photography and mixed media, these galleries feature works by both established and emerging artists. Take a leisurely stroll through these creative spaces, allowing yourself to be captivated by the beauty and talent on display.

The islands' local markets are a treasure trove of delights, offering an authentic glimpse into the local culture and community. Farmers, artists, and craftsmen come together to create a vibrant atmosphere where you can find an array of fresh produce, homemade preserves, handmade soaps, and more. Engage in friendly conversations with local vendors, who are often passionate about their craft and eager to share their knowledge and stories.

When it comes to accommodations, the San Juan Islands offer a diverse range of options to suit every traveler's needs and preferences. Cozy bed and breakfasts are scattered throughout the islands, providing a warm and welcoming atmosphere. Wake up to a delicious homemade breakfast prepared with local ingredients, and receive personalized recommendations from your hosts, who are often well-versed in the local attractions and hidden gems.

For those seeking a luxurious retreat, waterfront resorts and boutique hotels offer a slice of paradise. These establishments provide unparalleled views of the surrounding waters, upscale amenities, and exceptional service. Indulge in spa treatments, take a dip in a pool overlooking the ocean, or simply relax on your private balcony, immersing yourself in the tranquility of the islands.

For a more rustic experience, consider staying at a cabin or cottage nestled in the islands' natural beauty. These accommodations allow you to disconnect from the outside world and reconnect with nature. Wake up to the sound of birdsong, breathe in the fresh island air, and enjoy the peace and serenity that surrounds you. Campgrounds and RV parks cater to outdoor enthusiasts who want to immerse themselves in the islands' wilderness, providing a comfortable base for exploring the natural wonders of the San Juan Islands.

In conclusion, the San Juan Islands offer a delectable culinary adventure for food lovers. From fresh seafood and farm-to-table restaurants to cozy cafes and vibrant markets, the islands celebrate the region's rich culinary heritage. Indulge in the flavors of the Pacific Northwest, savoring mouthwatering delicacies made with locally sourced ingredients. Explore the unique shopping experiences, where you can discover one-of-a-kind souvenirs and handcrafted goods. And when it's time to rest, choose from a range of accommodations that cater to every taste and provide a comfortable and memorable stay. The San Juan Islands are truly a haven for those seeking exceptional cuisine, charming shopping, and unforgettable experiences.

Unique Shopping Experiences: Discover charming boutiques, art galleries, and local markets, offering one-of-a-kind souvenirs and handmade goods.

Immerse yourself in the vibrant arts and crafts scene of the San Juan Islands, where creativity and local talent flourish. The islands are home to a thriving community of artists, artisans, and craftsmen who draw inspiration from the stunning natural surroundings. As you explore the charming boutiques and specialty shops scattered across the islands, you'll discover a treasure trove of unique souvenirs, artisanal goods, and handcrafted treasures.

One of the highlights of the San Juan Islands' shopping scene is the exquisite jewelry made with locally sourced gemstones. Talented artisans meticulously craft intricate pieces that reflect the beauty of the islands. From delicate necklaces adorned with vibrant sea glass to stunning rings featuring rare gemstones found in the region, each piece tells a story of the islands' natural wonders. The jewelry designs often incorporate elements inspired by the marine life, coastal landscapes, and native flora, creating wearable art that captures the essence of the San Juan Islands.

Pottery is another art form that thrives in the island community. Skilled potters mold clay into beautiful and functional pieces, showcasing their craftsmanship and creativity. From elegant vases and decorative plates to unique coffee mugs and handmade tiles, the pottery created in the San Juan Islands reflects the rustic charm and organic beauty of the surroundings. Many artists offer workshops and demonstrations, allowing visitors to witness the intricate process of throwing clay on a wheel or hand-building ceramics.

The islands' artistic heritage also shines through in the handwoven textiles produced by local weavers. Using traditional techniques passed down through generations, these artisans create stunning fabrics and tapestries that showcase intricate patterns and vibrant colors. From scarves and shawls to blankets and rugs, the textiles are a testament to the skill and artistry of the weavers. These unique creations not only make for beautiful personal accessories and home décor items but also serve as a tangible connection to the islands' cultural heritage.

As you continue your exploration, be sure to visit the art galleries scattered throughout the San Juan Islands. These spaces serve as platforms for local artists to showcase their works, which encompass a diverse range of mediums and styles. You'll find paintings that capture the awe-inspiring landscapes of the islands, sculptures that evoke the spirit of nature, and photography that freezes moments of tranquility and wildlife encounters. The galleries provide an opportunity to engage with the artists themselves, learn about their inspiration, and perhaps even bring home a piece that resonates with you.

To truly immerse yourself in the local culture and support the island's artists and entrepreneurs, don't miss the opportunity to visit the lively local markets. These vibrant gatherings bring together farmers, artists, and craftsmen, offering an array of fresh produce, homemade preserves, handmade soaps, and much more. Stroll through the market stalls, sample delectable treats, and strike up conversations with the friendly vendors who are passionate about their crafts. Here, you can find locally grown fruits and vegetables bursting with flavor, artisanal cheeses crafted with care, and freshly baked goods that embody the essence of island life. The markets provide an authentic and immersive experience where you can interact with the local community and gain insights into the island's agricultural heritage.

One such market worth exploring is the San Juan Island Farmers Market, held every Saturday from April to October in the heart of Friday Harbor. Here, you'll find an abundance of organic produce, handmade crafts, and live music, creating a festive atmosphere that showcases the island's vibrant community spirit. The Orcas Island Artworks is another must-visit destination, located in the heart of Eastsound village. This cooperative gallery showcases the works of over 45 local artists, including paintings, ceramics, jewelry, and more. Browsing through the gallery feels like embarking on a visual journey through the island's creative landscape.

By immersing yourself in the arts and crafts scene of the San Juan Islands, you not only have the opportunity to find unique and meaningful souvenirs but also contribute to the local economy and support the livelihoods of talented artists and entrepreneurs. Each piece you acquire becomes a cherished memento of your time on the islands, carrying the spirit of the community and the natural beauty that surrounds it. Whether it's a handcrafted necklace, a hand-painted pottery piece, or a vibrant tapestry, these artistic treasures will serve as lasting reminders of your memorable visit to the San Juan Islands.

Accommodation Options: From cozy bed and breakfasts to waterfront resorts, find the perfect place to stay during your San Juan Islands getaway.

The San Juan Islands boast a wide range of accommodation options to suit every traveler's preferences and budget. Whether you're seeking a cozy bed and breakfast, a luxurious waterfront resort, a rustic cabin nestled in nature, or a campground for an outdoor adventure, the islands have something to offer for everyone.

Bed and breakfasts in the San Juan Islands provide a charming and intimate atmosphere, offering a home away from home. These cozy establishments are often run by friendly hosts who are passionate about providing personalized service to their guests. Wake up each morning to the tantalizing aroma of a delicious homemade breakfast prepared with fresh, local ingredients. Imagine savoring a plate of fluffy pancakes drizzled with maple syrup, accompanied by a side of crispy bacon sourced from a nearby farm. Your hosts will be more than happy to share their insider tips and recommendations, helping you make the most of your time on the islands. From the best hiking trails to secret beaches and hidden viewpoints, their local knowledge will enrich your experience and ensure you discover the hidden gems of the San Juan Islands.

For those seeking a luxurious retreat, waterfront resorts and boutique hotels offer an unparalleled experience. Picture yourself checking into a luxurious suite with panoramic views of the glistening waters, where every detail has been carefully curated to provide utmost comfort and relaxation.

Unwind with a rejuvenating spa treatment, indulge in a gourmet meal prepared by a renowned chef, or simply lounge by the pool while sipping a refreshing cocktail. The exceptional service and attention to detail in these upscale establishments will leave you feeling pampered and well-cared for. As the sun sets over the horizon, retire to your private balcony and soak in the breathtaking scenery, listening to the gentle lapping of the waves against the shore. These waterfront accommodations provide an idyllic setting for a romantic getaway or a special celebration, creating memories that will last a lifetime.

For a more rustic experience, consider staying in a cabin or cottage nestled in the island's natural beauty. These charming accommodations allow you to immerse yourself in the tranquility of nature while still enjoying modern comforts. Imagine waking up to the soft chirping of birds, stepping outside to breathe in the fresh island air, and sipping a cup of hot coffee as you watch the morning fog dissipate over the surrounding forest. Many of these cabins and cottages are tucked away in secluded spots, offering privacy and a sense of serenity. Take leisurely walks through the wooded trails, listen to the rustling of leaves as you explore the nearby parks, or simply curl up by the fireplace with a good book and a mug of hot cocoa. These rustic retreats provide the perfect opportunity to disconnect from the hustle and bustle of everyday life and reconnect with nature.

For outdoor enthusiasts and budget-conscious travelers, the San Juan Islands also offer a range of campgrounds and RV parks. Immerse yourself in the islands' wilderness by pitching a tent under the stars or parking your RV amidst towering trees. Campgrounds provide basic amenities such as restrooms, picnic tables, and fire pits, allowing you to enjoy a true outdoor experience. Fall asleep to the soothing sounds of nature, wake up to birdsong, and spend your days exploring the islands' hiking trails, kayaking along the coastline, or fishing in pristine waters. These campgrounds provide an affordable and immersive way to experience the natural wonders of the San Juan Islands.

In addition to the variety of accommodation options, the San Juan Islands also boast a vibrant dining scene, offering an array of culinary delights. After a day of exploration, treat yourself to a memorable dining experience at one of the many restaurants scattered across the islands. Indulge in fresh seafood caught that very day, savor farm-to-table dishes prepared with locally sourced ingredients, and sample wines from nearby vineyards. From quaint cafes serving homemade pastries to upscale restaurants with waterfront views, the culinary offerings in the San Juan Islands are sure to satisfy even the most discerning palates.

When it comes to shopping, the islands offer unique experiences that reflect the local culture and craftsmanship. Explore the charming boutiques and specialty shops, where you can find one-of-a-kind souvenirs and handcrafted goods. Browse through galleries that showcase a diverse range of artworks, including paintings, sculptures, ceramics, and jewelry created by talented local artists. Discover pieces that capture the essence of the islands' natural beauty or find a memento that will forever remind you of your time in this enchanting archipelago. Visit local markets where farmers, artists, and artisans come together to offer an array of fresh produce, handmade preserves, artisanal cheeses, and more. Engage with the local community, learn about their stories and traditions, and support independent businesses that contribute to the unique character of the San Juan Islands.

When it comes to finding and booking accommodation in the San Juan Islands, there are several popular apps and websites that can assist you in your search. Here are some widely used platforms:

Airbnb: Airbnb offers a wide range of accommodation options, including entire homes, private rooms, and shared spaces. You can filter your search based on location, price range, and specific amenities. Hosts in the San Juan Islands often provide unique and personalized experiences for their guests.

Booking.com: Booking.com is a popular online platform that offers a comprehensive selection of hotels, resorts, bed and breakfasts, and other types of accommodations. It provides detailed information about each property, including guest reviews, prices, and availability.

Expedia: Expedia is a well-known travel booking platform that allows you to search and compare a variety of accommodation options in the San Juan Islands. It offers a wide range of choices, from budget-friendly hotels to luxury resorts. You can also bundle your accommodations with flights and car rentals for additional savings.

Hotels.com: Hotels.com provides a user-friendly interface to search and book accommodations in the San Juan Islands. It offers a loyalty program where you can collect nights for future discounts. The platform provides detailed information about amenities, reviews, and photos to help you make an informed decision.

VRBO (Vacation Rentals by Owner): VRBO specializes in vacation rentals, including private homes, cottages, and cabins. It allows you to directly connect with property owners and offers a variety of filters to refine your search.

Many unique and picturesque properties can be found on this platform.

TripAdvisor: TripAdvisor is a popular travel website that provides comprehensive information on accommodations, restaurants, and attractions. It offers user-generated reviews and ratings for various properties, helping you make informed decisions. You can also find special deals and discounts on the platform.

Kayak: Kayak is a travel search engine that allows you to compare prices from different booking sites. It provides a wide range of accommodation options and offers useful filters to refine your search. You can also set price alerts to track any changes in rates.

HometoGo: HometoGo is a metasearch engine that aggregates vacation rental listings from various platforms, including Airbnb, VRBO, and Booking.com. It allows you to compare prices and availability across multiple sites, making it easier to find the best deals for your stay in the San Juan Islands.

These apps and websites offer convenience and flexibility in finding and booking accommodations in the San Juan Islands. Remember to read reviews, check the property details, and compare prices to ensure you find the best option that suits your preferences and budget.

In conclusion, the San Juan Islands offer a wealth of accommodation options that cater to diverse preferences and budgets. Whether you choose to stay in a cozy bed and breakfast, a luxurious waterfront resort, a rustic cabin, or a campground, you can be assured of a comfortable and memorable stay. The islands' rich culinary scene and unique shopping experiences further enhance your visit, providing opportunities to indulge in local flavors and discover handcrafted treasures. Whichever accommodation and activities you choose, the San Juan Islands will captivate you with their natural beauty, warm hospitality, and an abundance of unforgettable experiences.

Chapter 7: Planning and Resources

Travel Tips and Practical Information:

Currency:

An overview of the local currency, accepted payment methods, and tips for exchanging money or using ATMs on the islands.

The official currency in the San Juan Islands is the United States Dollar (USD). Most businesses, including hotels, restaurants, and shops, accept major credit cards such as Visa, Mastercard, and American Express. It is advisable to carry some cash for smaller establishments or in case of emergencies.

Exchanging currency can be done at banks or currency exchange offices in major cities before arriving on the islands. However, it's important to note that the availability of currency exchange services may be limited on the islands, so it is recommended to exchange money beforehand if needed.

ATMs can be found on the major islands, including Orcas Island, San Juan Island, and Lopez Island. These ATMs usually accept major bank cards, but it's advisable to check with your bank regarding any transaction fees or international withdrawal restrictions that may apply. Keep in mind that on smaller islands or more remote areas, ATMs may be scarce, so it's best to withdraw cash in advance.

It's also worth noting that while some businesses may accept Canadian currency, it is advisable to have US dollars for transactions in the San Juan Islands. Canadian coins, however, are not generally accepted.

Safety Tips:

Important guidelines for staying safe during your visit, including recommendations for outdoor activities, wildlife encounters, and water-based excursions.

The San Juan Islands offer a variety of outdoor activities, and ensuring your safety while enjoying these adventures is paramount. Here are some essential safety tips:

Hiking and Outdoor Activities:

Be prepared: Before heading out on a hike, make sure to research the trail, check the weather forecast, and carry appropriate gear such as sturdy footwear, extra clothing layers, sunscreen, and plenty of water.

Stay on marked trails: Straying from designated paths can be dangerous and harmful to the local ecosystem. Stick to established trails and respect any signage or closures.

Wildlife encounters: If you encounter wildlife, maintain a safe distance and observe them from afar. Never approach or feed wild animals, as it can be harmful to both you and the animals. Be particularly cautious around marine mammals, such as seals and sea lions, as they can become aggressive if they feel threatened.

Water-Based Activities:

Boating safety: If you plan to explore the islands by boat, familiarize yourself with navigation rules, ensure you have proper safety equipment on board, and check weather conditions before setting out. Let someone know about your plans and estimated return time.

Swimming and kayaking: When swimming or kayaking, always wear a life jacket, even if you are a strong swimmer. Be aware of tides and currents, especially in narrow channels and near rocky areas. It's also recommended to go with a buddy or let someone know about your water-based activities.

Emergency Preparedness:

Know the emergency numbers: Familiarize yourself with the local emergency contact numbers, including police, fire, and medical services.

Inform others: Share your travel plans with a trusted person, including your itinerary, contact information, and expected return time. This way, someone will be aware if you encounter any unexpected issues.

Weather conditions: Keep an eye on weather forecasts, especially if you plan to engage in outdoor activities. Sudden changes in weather can significantly impact your safety and should be taken into account when planning your itinerary.

Communication:

Information on mobile networks, Wi-Fi availability, and how to stay connected during your trip. Additionally, tips on emergency communication and local etiquette.

Mobile Networks and Wi-Fi Availability:

The San Juan Islands have decent mobile network coverage, particularly on the major islands. However, coverage may be spotty in more remote areas or on smaller islands. The major mobile service providers in the United States, such as AT&T,

Verizon, and T-Mobile, generally have coverage in the region.

Many accommodations, restaurants, and cafes offer free Wi-Fi for their customers, allowing you to stay connected during your trip. However, keep in mind that in more remote areas, Wi-Fi access may be limited or slower than in urban areas. It's a good idea to check with your accommodation provider regarding Wi-Fi availability and any potential usage restrictions.

Emergency Communication:

In case of emergencies, dial 911 to reach the appropriate emergency services in the San Juan Islands. Keep in mind that in more remote areas, it may take longer for emergency services to reach you, so it's important to be prepared and take necessary precautions for your safety.

Local Etiquette:

When visiting the San Juan Islands, it's helpful to familiarize yourself with local etiquette to ensure a respectful and enjoyable experience:

Respect nature and wildlife: The islands are known for their pristine natural beauty and diverse wildlife. Treat the environment with care, avoid littering, and follow any guidelines for wildlife encounters to minimize your impact on the ecosystem.

Be mindful of noise: The islands offer tranquility and a chance to connect with nature. Keep noise levels to a minimum, especially in residential areas and camping grounds, to respect the peaceful atmosphere.

Support local businesses: The San Juan Islands have a strong community of local businesses. Whenever possible, opt for locally-owned establishments, restaurants, and shops to support the local economy and experience the unique flavors and products of the islands.

Maps and Itineraries:

To maximize your time on the San Juan Islands and ensure you don't miss any highlights, customizable maps and suggested itineraries are invaluable resources.

Customizable Maps:

Detailed maps of the San Juan Islands are invaluable tools for exploring the diverse landscapes and attractions the islands have to offer. These maps can be obtained from visitor centers or downloaded from the official tourism websites, allowing you to conveniently access them before or during your trip.

The maps are designed to provide a comprehensive overview of the San Juan Islands, highlighting major attractions, hiking trails, beaches, and points of interest. With these maps in hand, you can easily navigate your way through the islands and customize your exploration to suit your specific interests and itinerary.

For outdoor enthusiasts, the maps showcase the extensive network of hiking trails that crisscross the islands. From the rugged and challenging terrains of Moran State Park on Orcas Island to the serene nature reserves on Lopez Island, there are trails suited for hikers of all levels. Whether you're seeking a leisurely stroll through the forest, a moderate hike to a scenic viewpoint, or a challenging ascent to a summit, the customizable maps allow you to select the trails that match your preferred difficulty level, distance, and scenic preferences. Each trail is marked with its length, elevation gain, and notable features, empowering you to make informed decisions based on your hiking abilities and interests.

If you have a fondness for sandy shores and the soothing sounds of the ocean, the maps highlight the pristine beaches along the coastlines of the San Juan Islands. From the well-known South Beach on San Juan Island to the hidden gem of Agate Beach on Lopez Island, you can easily customize your map to include the beaches you wish to explore. Each beach has its own unique charm, whether it's the abundance of seashells waiting to be collected, the opportunity for peaceful beachcombing along the shoreline, or the breathtaking views of the sunset painting the sky in vivid hues. With the help of the maps, you can plan beach-hopping adventures and mark the beaches that align with your preferences, ensuring you don't miss out on the coastal beauty the islands have to offer.

In addition to hiking trails and beaches, the maps also highlight the major attractions of the San Juan Islands. For history enthusiasts, the maps point out the locations of the historic English Camp and American Camp on San Juan Island. These sites offer a glimpse into the island's rich history and the contentious period known as the Pig War. You can immerse yourself in the stories of the past and explore the well-preserved remnants of the camps, including old buildings, interpretive exhibits, and scenic viewpoints.

Another prominent attraction highlighted on the maps is Lime Kiln Point State Park, also known as the "Whale Watch Park." This park is renowned for its prime whale-watching opportunities, particularly for spotting the majestic orcas that frequent the surrounding waters. By following the markers on the map, you can easily locate the best vantage points along the shoreline, where you can witness these magnificent creatures in their natural habitat. With the customizable maps, you can mark Lime Kiln Point State Park as a must-visit destination and ensure it's incorporated into your itinerary for a chance to witness these incredible marine mammals up close.

Suggested Itineraries:

To assist you in planning your trip, here are a few sample itineraries catering to different preferences and trip durations:

Outdoor Adventure Itinerary (3 Days):

Day 1: Arrive on San Juan Island, explore Friday Harbor, visit Lime Kiln Point State Park for whale watching, and enjoy dinner at a local seafood restaurant.

San Juan Island is the most populous of the San Juan Islands and serves as a vibrant hub for visitors. Upon arriving at the island, make your way to Friday Harbor, the island's charming main town. Stroll along the waterfront, perusing the boutiques, art galleries, and quaint shops that line the streets. Stop by the San Juan Islands Museum of Art to admire the local artistic talent.

For a breathtaking wildlife experience, head to Lime Kiln Point State Park, often referred to as the "Whale Watch Park." This park offers unparalleled views of the Salish Sea and is renowned as one of the best places in the world to observe orcas from the shoreline. Keep your eyes peeled for these majestic creatures as they swim, breach, and play in their natural habitat. The park also features informative interpretive panels that provide insights into the orcas' behavior and migration patterns.

As the day comes to a close, treat yourself to a delectable dinner at one of the local seafood restaurants. Indulge in freshly caught salmon, Dungeness crab, or succulent shellfish, paired with locally sourced produce and complemented by a selection of regional wines or craft beers. As you savor your meal, relish in the picturesque views of the harbor, the gentle lapping of the water, and the warm island ambiance.

Day 2: Take a ferry to Orcas Island, hike to the summit of Mount Constitution in Moran State Park, picnic by Cascade Lake, and end the day with a relaxing sunset kayak tour.

Catch an early morning ferry from San Juan Island to Orcas Island, known for its natural beauty and serene atmosphere. Once you arrive, embark on an exhilarating hike to the summit of Mount Constitution in Moran State Park. As you ascend through old-growth forests, be prepared to be rewarded with breathtaking panoramic views from the observation tower at the top. On a clear day, you can see the surrounding islands, snow-capped mountains, and even the Canadian mainland.

After your invigorating hike, make your way to Cascade Lake, a tranquil spot perfect for a leisurely picnic. Spread out a blanket by the lakeshore and enjoy a delightful lunch amidst nature's serenity. If you're feeling adventurous, rent a rowboat or paddleboard from the nearby rental facility and explore the calm waters of the lake.

As the sun starts to descend, embark on a memorable sunset kayak tour. Glide along the shimmering waters, guided by an experienced instructor who will lead you to the best vantage points for witnessing the vibrant colors of the setting sun. As the sky transforms into a canvas of fiery hues, take a moment to soak in the beauty and tranquility of the moment. The rhythmic paddling and the gentle lapping of the water create a meditative ambiance, making it a truly magical experience.

Day 3: Head to Lopez Island, rent a bike, and explore the island's scenic routes, stopping at various beaches and farm stands. In the afternoon, embark on a wildlife-watching boat tour before catching the ferry back to the mainland.

Take a short ferry ride from Orcas Island to Lopez Island, the "Friendly Isle" known for its laid-back atmosphere and idyllic pastoral landscapes. Rent a bike from one of the local shops and set off on a leisurely exploration of the island's scenic routes.

Lopez Island offers a network of quiet roads lined with picturesque farmlands, meandering coastlines, and breathtaking vistas. As you pedal along, take breaks at various beaches along the way, allowing yourself to bask in the tranquility and beauty of the surroundings. Some notable stops include Spencer Spit State Park, Shark Reef Sanctuary, and Iceberg Point.

Make sure to visit the island's charming farm stands, where you can sample fresh produce, artisanal cheeses, and other local delights. Lopez Island is renowned for its agricultural heritage, and the farm stands offer a glimpse into the island's commitment to sustainable farming practices and community-supported agriculture.

In the afternoon, embark on a wildlife-watching boat tour, providing an opportunity to encounter the abundant marine and birdlife of the Salish Sea. Keep your eyes peeled for seals, sea lions, porpoises, and a variety of seabirds that call these waters home. The experienced naturalist guides will offer informative commentary, enriching your understanding of the region's ecosystem and its inhabitants.

After the wildlife-watching tour, catch the ferry back to the mainland, cherishing the memories of your time on the San Juan Islands and contemplating the serene beauty you've experienced.

These suggested itineraries offer a glimpse into the diverse experiences that await you on the San Juan Islands. However, feel free to customize them according to your preferences, available time, and desired pace. The islands are a treasure trove of natural wonders, cultural gems, and culinary delights, ensuring a truly memorable journey.

Cultural Experience Itinerary (4 Days):

Day 1: Start on San Juan Island with visits to the San Juan Historical Museum and the Whale Museum. Enjoy a farm-to-table dinner showcasing local produce.

As you step foot on San Juan Island, immerse yourself in its rich history and vibrant cultural scene. Begin your journey by visiting the San Juan Historical Museum, located in the heart of Friday Harbor. This captivating museum takes you on a journey through time, showcasing the island's heritage through exhibits, artifacts, and engaging displays. Learn about the indigenous peoples who have called these islands home for thousands of years, the early European explorers who discovered the area, and the pioneers who shaped the island's development.

After delving into history, head to the Whale Museum, a must-visit destination for anyone fascinated by marine life. This unique museum is dedicated to the study and conservation of whales in the Salish Sea. Explore the interactive exhibits, listen to the mesmerizing songs of whales, and gain a deeper understanding of these majestic creatures. Discover the ongoing research efforts and conservation initiatives aimed at protecting the diverse marine ecosystem of the San Juan Islands.

In the evening, treat your taste buds to a farm-to-table dinner, savoring the flavors of the San Juan Islands. With its fertile land and abundant local produce, the islands boast a vibrant culinary scene. Enjoy dishes prepared with freshly harvested ingredients sourced from nearby farms. Indulge in succulent seafood caught just off the island's shores, taste the sweetness of locally grown berries, and savor the rich flavors of artisanal cheeses and wines. Whether you choose a cozy waterfront restaurant or a quaint farm-to-table eatery, the emphasis on freshness and quality will leave a lasting impression.

Day 2: Take a ferry to Lopez Island and immerse yourself in the island's arts scene by visiting local galleries and studios. Explore the charming village of Lopez Village and indulge in a culinary tour of the island's renowned restaurants.

Hop on a ferry and venture to the tranquil Lopez Island, renowned for its thriving arts community and serene landscapes. As you disembark, you'll immediately sense the creative energy that permeates the island. Start your day by visiting the local galleries and studios that showcase the diverse artistic talents of Lopez Island's residents. From painters and sculptors to potters and jewelers, you'll have the opportunity to admire and even purchase unique pieces of art that reflect the island's natural beauty and creative spirit.

After immersing yourself in the arts, wander through the charming village of Lopez Village. This idyllic waterfront town exudes a laid-back atmosphere, inviting you to explore its boutique shops, bookstores, and quaint cafes. Take your time to browse for handmade crafts, locally crafted goods, and one-of-a-kind souvenirs that capture the essence of the island.

No visit to Lopez Island is complete without indulging in its culinary delights. Embark on a culinary tour, sampling the island's renowned restaurants and eateries. From farm-to-table establishments to cozy seaside cafes, each venue offers a unique dining experience. Relish in the flavors of dishes prepared with fresh, locally sourced ingredients, from succulent seafood platters to mouthwatering vegetarian delights. Pair your meal with a glass of locally produced wine or craft beer, further enhancing the sensory journey.

Day 3: Return to San Juan Island and spend the day visiting historical sites such as the English Camp and the Pelindaba Lavender Farm. Enjoy a performance at the San Juan Community Theatre in the evening.

Return to San Juan Island and dedicate the day to exploring its historical sites and natural beauty. Start by visiting the English Camp, a captivating historical site that takes you back to the mid-19th century. This former British military encampment played a crucial role in the border dispute between the United States and Great Britain. Stroll through the preserved buildings, wander along the trails, and immerse yourself in the stories of the past. Admire the picturesque landscapes surrounding the camp, providing a glimpse into the historical significance and natural beauty of the island.

Continue your journey with a visit to the Pelindaba Lavender Farm, where fragrant fields of purple await. Explore the lavender farm's picturesque grounds, breathe in the soothing aroma, and learn about the various uses and benefits of lavender. Discover the art of lavender distillation, witness the creation of lavender-infused products, and indulge in a sensory experience like no other. Browse the farm's gift shop for lavender-inspired souvenirs, essential oils, and culinary treats.

In the evening, immerse yourself in the vibrant performing arts scene at the San Juan Community Theatre. This intimate venue showcases a variety of performances, including theater productions, live music concerts, dance performances, and comedy shows. Take a seat and allow yourself to be transported into a world of creativity and talent. Whether it's a local production or a visiting artist, the performances at the San Juan Community Theatre never fail to captivate audiences.

Day 4: Discover the artistic vibe of Orcas Island by exploring Eastsound, browsing art galleries, and attending a local festival or event. End your cultural journey with a sunset beach picnic.

Embark on a scenic journey to Orcas Island, known for its breathtaking landscapes and thriving arts community. Begin your exploration in Eastsound, the island's charming main village. Stroll through the streets lined with art galleries, showcasing an array of artistic styles and mediums. From contemporary paintings and sculptures to handmade crafts and jewelry, the galleries offer a glimpse into the island's artistic vibe. Engage with the local artists, learn about their creative processes, and perhaps find a piece of art that speaks to you.

Immerse yourself further in the island's cultural scene by attending a local festival or event, if one happens to coincide with your visit. Orcas Island hosts a variety of lively festivals throughout the year, celebrating music, art, food, and community. From music festivals that showcase local talent to art walks that invite visitors to explore the island's creative spaces, these events provide a unique opportunity to experience the vibrant spirit of Orcas Island.

As the day draws to a close, savor a truly magical experience with a sunset beach picnic. Orcas Island offers numerous picturesque beaches where you can witness the sun sinking below the horizon, casting vibrant hues across the sky. Select a secluded spot, spread out a blanket, and indulge in a picnic featuring local gourmet treats. As you enjoy the delectable flavors, listen to the soothing sound of the waves and feel the gentle sea breeze on your skin. Let the beauty of Orcas Island's nature and artistry merge into a transcendent moment.

These sample itineraries provide a glimpse into the diverse experiences and enchanting destinations the San Juan Islands have to offer. Customize them according to your preferences, time availability, and desired pace, and get ready to embark on a journey that combines history, culture, nature, and art, creating memories that will last a lifetime.

Relaxation and Wellness Itinerary (5 Days):

Day 1: Arrive on Lopez Island and check into a tranquil waterfront resort. Unwind with a massage or spa treatment and savor a leisurely dinner overlooking the serene waters.

As you step off the ferry onto Lopez Island, you immediately sense the laid-back and serene atmosphere that permeates the island. Make your way to one of the island's waterfront resorts, nestled along the picturesque coastline, and check into your cozy accommodation. Take a moment to breathe in the fresh sea air and appreciate the stunning views that surround you.

To truly embrace the relaxation and rejuvenation that the San Juan Islands offer, treat yourself to a soothing massage or spa treatment at the resort. Indulge in a blissful hour of pampering as skilled therapists melt away any residual stress, leaving you feeling refreshed and rejuvenated.

As the sun begins to set, head to the resort's restaurant or venture into Lopez Village for a memorable dining experience. Lopez Island boasts a thriving farm-to-table culinary scene, where chefs incorporate fresh, locally sourced ingredients into their creations. Savor delectable seafood dishes, accompanied by a glass of Washington State wine, as you enjoy the tranquil ambiance and the gentle sounds of the waves lapping against the shore.

Day 2: Take a scenic hike through Spencer Spit State Park, enjoy a beachside yoga session, and indulge in a farm-fresh picnic lunch. Spend the afternoon strolling through the Lopez Village shops and treating yourself to local ice cream.

Start your day with a hearty breakfast at a local café in Lopez Village, fueling up for the adventures that lie ahead. Lace up your hiking boots and make your way to Spencer Spit State Park, known for its picturesque sandy spit that stretches out into the Salish Sea. As you wander along the trails, you'll be immersed in the island's natural beauty, surrounded by lush forests, vibrant wildflowers, and stunning views of the water.

After your hike, find a serene spot on the beach for a yoga session. As you flow through poses, the rhythmic sound of the waves and the gentle sea breeze create a tranquil and meditative atmosphere, allowing you to connect with nature on a deeper level.

For lunch, indulge in a farm-fresh picnic at one of the park's designated picnic areas. Visit a local farm stand or the Lopez Island Farmers Market to gather an assortment of delicious, locally sourced goodies, such as artisanal cheeses, freshly baked bread, vibrant fruits, and organic vegetables. As you savor each bite, take in the panoramic views of the water and appreciate the simple pleasures of island life.

In the afternoon, meander through Lopez Village, a charming hub of boutiques, galleries, and specialty shops.

Browse through unique handcrafted jewelry, locally made pottery, and vibrant works of art, all created by talented island artisans. As you explore the village, treat yourself to a scoop of homemade ice cream from one of the local shops, savoring the flavors of the San Juan Islands with each creamy spoonful.

Day 3: Journey to Orcas Island and immerse yourself in the island's natural beauty by visiting the beautiful Doe Bay Resort. Relax in hot springs, rejuvenate with a yoga class, and pamper yourself with a spa session.

Today, hop on a ferry to Orcas Island, known for its awe-inspiring landscapes and tranquil atmosphere. As you disembark, the towering evergreen trees and rugged coastline beckon you to explore the island's natural wonders.

Head to Doe Bay Resort, a hidden gem nestled on the eastern shore of Orcas Island. This eco-friendly retreat offers a blend of relaxation, wellness, and breathtaking views of the Salish Sea. Begin your day by soaking in the resort's natural hot springs. As you dip into the warm mineral-rich waters, surrounded by lush vegetation and the sounds of nature, feel your worries melt away. The therapeutic properties of the hot springs provide both physical and mental rejuvenation, leaving you feeling refreshed and invigorated.

After your hot springs experience, participate in a rejuvenating yoga class. Doe Bay Resort offers various yoga sessions, from gentle flow to challenging vinyasa, catering to practitioners of all levels. Allow the peaceful surroundings to enhance your practice as you find balance and serenity amidst the island's natural beauty.

To further indulge in relaxation, treat yourself to a spa session at Doe Bay's Healing Arts Center. Skilled therapists provide a range of wellness treatments, including massages, facials, and body wraps, using organic and locally sourced products. Surrender to the healing touch of the therapists and let the tranquil ambiance of the center envelop you in a state of bliss.

Day 4: Return to San Juan Island and explore the tranquil beaches of South Beach and Cattle Point. Treat yourself to a sunset sailboat cruise and a romantic dinner overlooking the water.

Bid farewell to Orcas Island and catch the ferry back to San Juan Island, where new adventures await. As you arrive, feel the serene energy of the island envelop you once again. Start your exploration by visiting the tranquil beaches of South Beach and Cattle Point, located on the southern tip of the island.

South Beach, known for its expansive sandy shoreline, offers breathtaking views of the Strait of Juan de Fuca and the Olympic Mountains. Take a leisurely stroll along the beach, letting the soft sand massage your feet as you listen to the gentle crashing of the waves. Look out for sea lions basking on the rocks and bald eagles soaring overhead, showcasing the abundant wildlife that thrives in this pristine coastal environment.

Continuing along the coastline, make your way to Cattle Point, where rugged cliffs and dramatic sea stacks provide a dramatic backdrop. Enjoy the solitude and serenity of this picturesque spot, taking in the panoramic views of the ocean and the distant islands.

In the evening, embark on a romantic sunset sailboat cruise, allowing you to witness the breathtaking colors of the sky as the sun dips below the horizon. Sail along the tranquil waters, feeling the gentle breeze on your face and the warmth of the setting sun on your skin. Toast to the beauty of the San Juan Islands with a glass of sparkling wine, creating a lasting memory of this enchanting place.

Conclude your day with a romantic dinner at one of the island's waterfront restaurants. Indulge in the fresh flavors of the sea as you feast on locally caught seafood delicacies, accompanied by a bottle of fine Washington State wine. As you savor each bite, watch as the lights from nearby boats shimmer on the water, creating a magical ambiance that perfectly complements your unforgettable dining experience.

Day 5: Spend your final day on San Juan Island by visiting the Lavender Wind Farm, enjoying a wine tasting at a local vineyard, and taking a leisurely stroll through Roche Harbor's charming marina.

On your final day in the San Juan Islands, make the most of your time on San Juan Island by exploring its unique attractions and scenic beauty.

Start your day with a visit to the Lavender Wind Farm, located on the island's west side. Immerse yourself in the sight and scent of vibrant lavender fields, as the fragrant blooms dance in the breeze. Take a leisurely stroll through the farm, learning about the cultivation and distillation of lavender and its many uses. Visit the farm's gift shop, where you can purchase a variety of lavender-infused products, from essential oils and soaps to culinary delights and decorative items. Capture the essence of the San Juan Islands by taking home a souvenir that encapsulates the tranquility and beauty of the lavender farm.

Continue your journey by indulging in a wine tasting experience at one of the island's local vineyards. San Juan

Island has a growing reputation for producing exceptional wines, thanks to its unique climate and fertile soil. Visit a vineyard and savor the flavors of handcrafted wines, learning about the winemaking process from passionate vintners. Allow your taste buds to dance as you sample a variety of varietals, from crisp whites to bold reds, each reflecting the distinct character of the island.

As the day unfolds, make your way to Roche Harbor, a charming marina village on the northern tip of the island. Take a leisurely stroll along the harbor, admiring the collection of sailboats and yachts moored along the docks. Explore the quaint shops and boutiques, where you can find unique treasures and local artisan crafts. Pause to admire the historic Hotel de Haro, a century-old hotel that exudes timeless elegance and rich history. Enjoy a leisurely dinner at one of the waterfront restaurants, as you soak in the peaceful ambiance and the captivating views of the marina.

As you bid farewell to the San Juan Islands, reflect on the moments of relaxation, adventure, and natural beauty that have defined your journey. The memories you've created and the experiences you've cherished will linger in your heart, serving as a reminder of the remarkable allure of the San Juan Islands.

These suggested itineraries provide a starting point for planning your visit to the San Juan Islands, and you can customize them further based on your interests, available time, and desired pace.

Useful Contacts and Websites:

Visitor Centers:

One of the first stops you should make upon arriving in the San Juan Islands is the visitor centers located on each major island. These centers serve as valuable resources for travelers, offering a wealth of information, maps, brochures, and expert advice on planning your activities. Whether you need directions, recommendations, or want to learn more about the local history and attractions, the knowledgeable staff at the visitor centers are there to assist you.

San Juan Island Visitor Center:

Location: 10 First Street, Friday Harbor, San Juan Island

Contact: Phone: (360) 378-9551 | Website: www.visitsanjuans.com

The San Juan Island Visitor Center, located in the heart of Friday Harbor, is a great starting point for your island adventure. Here, you can find detailed maps, brochures, and up-to-date information on the island's attractions, events, and services. The friendly staff is always ready to provide personalized recommendations based on your interests, whether it's exploring historical sites like American Camp and English Camp, visiting the renowned Lime Kiln Point State Park for whale watching, or discovering the vibrant art scene in the area.

Orcas Island Chamber of Commerce & Visitor Center:

Location: 65 North Beach Road, Eastsound, Orcas Island

Contact: Phone: (360) 376-2273 | Website: www.visitsanjuans.com

The Orcas Island Chamber of Commerce & Visitor Center is your gateway to discovering the wonders of Orcas Island. The center offers a range of resources, including maps, brochures, and insider tips on hiking trails, water activities, and local events. Whether you're interested in exploring Moran State Park with its breathtaking vistas, enjoying a scenic drive along the island's picturesque coastline, or indulging in the island's culinary delights, the knowledgeable staff can help you plan an unforgettable Orcas Island experience.

Lopez Island Visitor Center:

Location: 521 Bakerview Road, Lopez Island

Contact: Phone: (360) 468-4664 | Website: www.visitsanjuans.com

The Lopez Island Visitor Center welcomes you to the serene and laid-back atmosphere of Lopez Island. Here, you can obtain maps, brochures, and insider advice on the island's hidden gems, including tranquil beaches, scenic biking routes, and charming local farms. The helpful staff can guide you to places like Spencer Spit State Park, where you can enjoy birdwatching and beachcombing, or recommend a visit to the Lopez Island Historical Museum to learn about the island's fascinating history. Whether you're seeking a peaceful retreat or outdoor adventures, the visitor center is an excellent resource for planning your Lopez Island experience.

Tour Operators:

For those seeking guided excursions and specialized experiences in the San Juan Islands, there are several reputable tour operators available. These tour operators offer a range of activities, such as whale watching tours, kayaking trips, and scenic cruises, providing you with the opportunity to explore the islands' natural wonders while learning from knowledgeable guides. Here are a few recommended tour operators to consider:

San Juan Safaris:

Contact: Phone: (800) 450-6858 | Website: www.sanjuansafaris.com

San Juan Safaris specializes in whale watching tours, offering thrilling opportunities to witness orcas, humpback whales, seals, and other marine life in their natural habitat. With experienced naturalist guides and comfortable vessels equipped with viewing decks, their tours provide an educational and immersive experience. Prepare to be amazed as you witness these majestic creatures up close while learning about their behaviors and conservation efforts.

Outer Island Expeditions:

Contact: Phone: (360) 376-3711 | Website: www.outerislandx.com

Outer Island Expeditions offers a variety of guided tours, including whale watching, sea kayaking, and wildlife cruises. Embark on a journey to encounter orcas, seals, eagles, and other wildlife in their pristine island habitats. Their knowledgeable guides share insights about the area's ecology and natural history, making each excursion informative and exciting. Whether you choose to paddle through scenic waterways or cruise along the coastline, Outer Island Expeditions offers unforgettable experiences for nature enthusiasts.

Shearwater Kayak Tours:

Contact: Phone: (360) 376-4699 | Website: www.shearwaterkayaks.com

For those interested in exploring the San Juan Islands by kayak, Shearwater Kayak Tours provides expertly guided trips catering to all skill levels. From half-day paddles to multi-day expeditions, their tours allow you to discover secluded coves, rocky shorelines, and hidden beaches. Experience the tranquility of gliding through the water, observing marine life, and soaking in the breathtaking scenery. With knowledgeable guides ensuring your safety and providing fascinating insights, Shearwater Kayak Tours is an excellent choice for a unique and eco-friendly adventure.

Online Platforms:

In addition to visitor centers and tour operators, there are numerous online platforms that can enhance your exploration of the San Juan Islands. These platforms offer a wealth of information, insights, and recommendations from both locals and fellow travelers. Here are some useful websites and online platforms to assist you in planning your trip:

Visit San Juans - Official Tourism Website:

Website: www.visitsanjuans.com

The official tourism website for the San Juan Islands is a comprehensive resource that provides an overview of the islands, including information on attractions, accommodations, dining, events, and transportation options. It offers up-to-date details on island activities, allowing you to tailor your itinerary and make the most of your visit.

San Juan Islands Insider:

Website: www.sanjuanislandsinsider.com

San Juan Islands Insider is a locally-run blog that showcases the hidden gems, unique experiences, and insider tips of the islands. From lesser-known hiking trails to local events and culinary delights, this blog offers an insider's perspective on making the most of your time in the San Juans.

San Juan Islands Community Forums:

Website: www.sanjuanislandforums.com

The San Juan Islands Community Forums provide a platform for travelers to engage with locals, ask questions, and seek recommendations. From discussing the best spots for wildlife photography to sharing recent experiences, this online community is a valuable resource for gathering insights and connecting with fellow visitors.

By utilizing the visitor centers, contacting reputable tour operators, and exploring online platforms, you can gather the necessary information, expert advice, and local recommendations to ensure a memorable and well-planned visit to the San Juan Islands.

Chapter 8: Practical Information

In this chapter, you will find all the essential travel tips, accommodation options, and transportation details you need to plan your trip to the San Juan Islands.

Travel Tips:

When to Visit: The San Juan Islands can be visited year-round, offering unique experiences and breathtaking beauty in every season. However, the peak tourist season occurs during the summer months, from June to August, when the islands come alive with visitors from all over the world. During this time, you can expect vibrant festivals, bustling farmers markets, and a wide range of outdoor activities to enjoy. If you're looking for a quieter and more intimate experience, it's recommended to visit during the shoulder seasons of spring (April to May) or fall (September to October).

Spring in the San Juan Islands brings a burst of colorful blossoms and the awakening of nature. The islands become a paradise for birdwatchers as migratory birds return, filling the air with their melodic songs. The weather during spring is generally mild, with occasional rain showers. It's a great time to explore the islands' hiking trails, witness wildflowers in bloom, and participate in local events such as the Annual Artists' Studio Tour, where artists open their studios to the public.

Fall, on the other hand, is a time of tranquility and stunning natural beauty. As the summer crowds disperse, the islands embrace a peaceful atmosphere. The foliage transforms into a mesmerizing palette of warm hues, creating a picturesque setting for hiking, biking, and scenic drives. Fall is also the time for harvest festivals and culinary delights, with local farms offering fresh produce and farm-to-table dining experiences. Don't miss the Lopez Island Vineyards Harvest Festival, where you can indulge in wine tasting and vineyard tours.

Weather Conditions: The San Juan Islands enjoy a mild maritime climate, influenced by the surrounding waters of the Salish Sea. Summers are generally warm and pleasant, with average temperatures ranging from 65°F to 75°F (18°C to 24°C). The days are long, providing ample daylight hours to explore and enjoy outdoor activities. However, it's important to note that the weather can be variable, and it's wise to pack layers to accommodate temperature changes throughout the day.

Winters in the San Juan Islands are cool and wet, but they possess a unique charm. The islands' natural beauty takes on a serene and ethereal quality, with misty mornings and dramatic coastal scenes. The temperatures range from 40°F to 50°F (4°C to 10°C), and rainfall is common. While outdoor activities may be limited during this season, it's an ideal time for cozying up in front of a fireplace, savoring local cuisine, and exploring the islands' cultural attractions.

Packing Suggestions: To make the most of your San Juan Islands adventure, there are a few essential items to include in your packing list:

Sunscreen: Even on cloudy days, the sun's rays can be strong, so be sure to pack sunscreen to protect your skin.

Insect Repellent: Mosquitoes and other insects can be present, especially in wooded areas or during dusk and dawn. Having insect repellent on hand will ensure a more comfortable outdoor experience.

Reusable Water Bottle: Staying hydrated is essential, and having a reusable water bottle allows you to refill it throughout your explorations while reducing plastic waste.

Comfortable Walking Shoes: The islands offer numerous opportunities for walking, hiking, and exploring. Bring comfortable shoes that are suitable for various terrains, such as trails, beaches, and village streets.

Waterproof Jacket: Given the islands' maritime climate, rain showers are common throughout the year. A waterproof jacket will keep you dry and comfortable during outdoor activities.

Layered Clothing: Due to the variability in weather, it's advisable to pack clothing that can be layered. This allows you to adjust your attire according to temperature changes throughout the day.

Outdoor Activity Gear: If you plan to engage in activities like hiking, kayaking, or wildlife viewing, consider packing a daypack, binoculars, a hat for sun protection, and sturdy footwear suitable for the terrain.

By considering these suggestions, you'll be well-prepared to embrace the beauty and diversity of the San Juan Islands, regardless of the season. Remember to check the local weather forecast before your trip and make any necessary adjustments to your packing list to ensure a comfortable and enjoyable stay.

Accommodation Options:

The San Juan Islands offer a range of accommodation options to suit different preferences and budgets:

Bed and Breakfasts:

The San Juan Islands are known for their cozy and charming bed and breakfast establishments, offering visitors a warm and personalized experience. Scattered across the islands, these accommodations provide a unique opportunity to connect with the local community and enjoy the island life. Each bed and breakfast has its own distinctive character, often reflecting the natural beauty and laid-back atmosphere of the San Juans.

Staying at a bed and breakfast allows you to immerse yourself in the local culture and hospitality. The hosts are typically residents of the islands and are knowledgeable about the best places to explore, dine, and relax. They can offer insider tips and recommendations, helping you make the most of your visit. Many bed and breakfasts pride themselves on creating a welcoming and homey atmosphere, making you feel like a part of the island community.

One of the highlights of staying at a bed and breakfast is the homemade breakfast that is often included. Imagine waking up to the aroma of freshly brewed coffee and enjoying a delicious meal prepared with local ingredients. From fluffy pancakes topped with berries picked from the nearby farms to savory omelets filled with locally sourced seafood, breakfast at a bed and breakfast is a delightful way to start your day of island adventures.

Resorts and Hotels:

For those seeking a more luxurious and indulgent stay, the San Juan Islands offer a selection of waterfront resorts and hotels. These accommodations provide breathtaking views of the surrounding waters, elegant amenities, and convenient access to the islands' attractions. Whether you're looking for a romantic getaway or a pampering retreat, the resorts and hotels in the San Juans aim to provide a memorable experience.

The waterfront resorts in the San Juan Islands are designed to take full advantage of the natural beauty that surrounds them. You can wake up to stunning sunrises over the water, lounge on private balconies while enjoying the gentle sea breeze, or relax in luxurious spas offering rejuvenating treatments. Some resorts also offer outdoor activities such as kayaking, boating, or whale watching tours, allowing you to explore the islands' natural wonders with ease.

Hotels in the towns and villages of the San Juan Islands provide a range of options, from boutique hotels to well-known chains. These accommodations offer comfortable rooms, convenient amenities, and proximity to local restaurants, shops, and attractions. Whether you're looking for a place to unwind after a day of exploration or a base for your island adventures, hotels provide a convenient and comfortable option.

Vacation Rentals:

If you prefer a home-away-from-home experience, vacation rentals in the San Juan Islands offer an ideal solution. Cottages, cabins, beach houses, and other types of vacation rentals can be found throughout the islands, providing space, privacy, and the freedom to create your own schedule. These rentals are particularly popular for families, groups of friends, or couples seeking a romantic retreat.

Renting a vacation home allows you to fully immerse yourself in the island lifestyle. You can enjoy the comforts of a fully equipped kitchen, where you can prepare meals using local produce and seafood from the island's markets. Many vacation rentals come with outdoor spaces such as decks, gardens, or private beaches, where you can relax, barbecue, or simply soak in the tranquil surroundings.

The variety of vacation rentals available in the San Juan Islands ensures that there is something to suit every taste and budget. Whether you're looking for a cozy cabin nestled in the woods, a beachfront cottage with panoramic ocean views, or a spacious house for a large group gathering, you can find the perfect vacation rental that meets your needs and preferences.

Camping and RV Parks:

For nature enthusiasts and outdoor lovers, camping in the San Juan Islands is an excellent way to immerse yourself in the pristine beauty of the archipelago. Several campgrounds and RV parks are available on the islands, providing facilities and amenities for a comfortable camping experience.

Camping in the San Juans allows you to wake up surrounded by nature, with the sound of birds chirping and the scent of pine trees in the air. The campgrounds offer a range of options, from tent sites to RV hookups, accommodating different camping preferences. Some campgrounds provide amenities such as picnic areas, fire pits, restrooms, and showers to enhance your camping experience.

Immersing yourself in the natural surroundings of the San Juan Islands through camping allows for easy access to outdoor activities such as hiking, birdwatching, beachcombing, and stargazing. Many campgrounds are located near hiking trails, where you can explore the islands' diverse ecosystems and enjoy panoramic views of the surrounding landscapes. Additionally, camping provides opportunities for campfire gatherings, storytelling, and connecting with fellow campers, fostering a sense of community and shared experiences.

It's important to note that due to the popularity of camping in the San Juans, reservations are often recommended, especially during peak travel seasons. Planning ahead and securing your campsite in advance will ensure a smooth and enjoyable camping experience.

When it comes to finding and booking accommodation in the San Juan Islands, several popular apps and websites can help simplify the process. Here are a few widely used platforms for locating and securing your desired lodging:

Airbnb: Airbnb offers a wide range of vacation rentals, including cottages, cabins, and unique properties, allowing you to stay in the heart of the San Juan Islands. The platform provides user reviews, photos, and detailed descriptions to help you make an informed decision.

Booking.com: Known for its extensive global reach, Booking.com also features a variety of accommodations in the San Juan Islands. From bed and breakfasts to hotels and resorts, the platform provides user ratings, flexible search filters, and competitive pricing options.

Expedia: Expedia is a popular online travel agency that allows you to search for and book accommodation options in the San Juan Islands. The platform provides a comprehensive selection of hotels, resorts, and vacation rentals, along with customer reviews and competitive rates.

VRBO (Vacation Rentals by Owner): VRBO specializes in vacation rentals and offers a range of properties in the San Juan Islands. With detailed property descriptions, photos, and guest reviews, VRBO allows you to find and book the perfect vacation rental for your stay.

TripAdvisor: In addition to its extensive collection of travel information and reviews, TripAdvisor also offers a booking feature for accommodations. With user-generated reviews, ratings, and price comparisons, it can help you find suitable options for your stay in the San Juan Islands.

Hotels.com: As the name suggests, Hotels.com is a platform dedicated to hotel bookings worldwide. It provides a variety of hotel options in the San Juan Islands, with detailed information, user reviews, and competitive rates.

Kayak: Kayak is a comprehensive travel search engine that allows you to compare prices across multiple platforms, including hotels, vacation rentals, and other accommodation options. It provides a user-friendly interface, making it easy to find and book accommodation in the San Juan Islands.

It's important to note that availability and pricing may vary depending on the season and demand, so it's advisable to book your accommodation well in advance, especially during peak travel periods in the San Juan Islands. Additionally, it's always a good idea to read reviews, compare prices, and consider the location and amenities offered by each property before making your final booking decision.

Whether you choose a cozy bed and breakfast, a luxurious waterfront resort, a charming vacation rental, or a camping adventure, the San Juan Islands offer a range of accommodation options to suit every traveler's preferences. Whichever type of accommodation you select, you'll have the opportunity to immerse yourself in the natural beauty, warm hospitality, and unique experiences that the San Juans have to offer.

Transportation Details:

Getting to the San Juan Islands and getting around the archipelago requires some planning. Here are the transportation options to consider:

Ferry Services:

The most convenient and popular way to reach the San Juan Islands is through the Washington State Ferries. These ferries operate from the town of Anacortes, located on the mainland, and provide regular service to several islands, including Orcas Island, San Juan Island, and Lopez Island.

Ferry schedules can vary depending on the season, so it's important to check the schedules in advance to plan your trip accordingly. During peak travel seasons, such as summer weekends or holidays, the ferries can get quite busy. To secure your spot, it is advisable to make reservations, especially if you are traveling with a vehicle. Reservations can be made online or by phone, and it is recommended to do so well in advance, particularly for popular departure times.

The ferry journey itself offers a scenic and enjoyable experience. As you sail through the Salish Sea, you can marvel at the stunning views of the surrounding waters and the rugged coastline. Keep your eyes peeled for wildlife sightings, including whales, seals, and seabirds, which are not uncommon during the crossing.

Private Boat Rentals:

For those who prefer a more independent mode of transportation and have boating experience, private boat rentals provide an excellent option for exploring the San Juan Islands at your own pace. Several marinas and rental agencies offer a variety of boats, including powerboats, sailboats, and kayaks, catering to different preferences and skill levels.

Before embarking on your private boating adventure, it is crucial to familiarize yourself with local navigation rules and safety precautions. Ensure you have the necessary boating licenses and permits, as required, and be aware of any specific regulations governing the waters around the islands. It is also advisable to check weather conditions and tides before setting out, as the waters in the region can be unpredictable.

Having your own boat allows you the freedom to visit remote coves and bays, discover hidden beaches, and explore the islands' pristine coastline. You can create your own itinerary, hopping from island to island, and spend as much time as you desire at each location. Just remember to respect the natural environment, follow any local regulations, and practice responsible boating to preserve the beauty of the San Juan Islands.

Inter-Island Transportation:

Once you have arrived on the San Juan Islands, there are various options available for inter-island transportation, making it easy to navigate between different islands and explore their unique offerings.

Shuttle Buses: Inter-island shuttle buses operate on some of the major islands, providing a convenient and cost-effective means of transportation. These shuttles typically run on fixed schedules, connecting key locations and attractions, such as ferry terminals, towns, and popular landmarks. They offer a hassle-free way to move around, especially if you prefer not to drive or rent a vehicle.

Taxis: Taxis are another option for getting around the islands. They can be found at ferry terminals or can be called for pickup. Taxis provide a more personalized and direct service, allowing you to reach specific destinations without the need to navigate or worry about parking.

Rental Cars: If you prefer the freedom and flexibility of having your own vehicle, rental cars are available on the islands. It's recommended to reserve a rental car in advance, especially during peak travel seasons, to ensure availability. Having a car allows you to explore the islands at your own pace and access more remote areas that may be less accessible by public transportation.

Bicycles: The San Juan Islands are known for being bicycle-friendly, with scenic roads and bike lanes that provide a unique way to explore the islands' natural beauty. Many towns and rental shops offer bicycles for rent, including electric bikes, allowing you to enjoy leisurely rides along coastal routes, visit local farms, or access hidden trails. Bicycles also provide an eco-friendly and healthy transportation option, immersing you in the sights, sounds, and scents of the islands.

Regardless of which inter-island transportation option you choose, it's essential to plan your routes and consider the time it takes to travel between islands. While the distances are relatively short, factors such as ferry schedules, traffic, and waiting times can impact your overall travel time. It's a good idea to allocate ample time for transportation, ensuring you have enough time to fully explore each island and make the most of your San Juan Islands adventure.

Remember to always follow local transportation regulations, respect the environment, and prioritize safety when traveling between islands. By utilizing the ferry services, private boat rentals, and inter-island transportation options available, you can navigate the San Juan Islands with ease and embark on unforgettable experiences throughout this picturesque archipelago.

By considering these practical tips and information, you'll be well-prepared to make the most of your trip to the beautiful San Juan Islands.

Chapter 9: Insider Recommendations

In this chapter, we bring you the insider recommendations from locals and seasoned travelers who have experienced the San Juan Islands firsthand. These recommendations will guide you to discover hidden gems, explore local secrets, and engage in lesser-known activities that will make your trip truly memorable.

Hidden Gems and Local Secrets:

The San Juan Islands are renowned for their natural beauty and picturesque landscapes, but beyond the well-known attractions, there are hidden gems and local secrets waiting to be discovered. Let's take a closer look at three of these lesser-known treasures: Olga on Orcas Island, Watmough Bay on Lopez Island, and the Shaw Island Historical Museum.

Nestled on the eastern side of Orcas Island, the charming village of Olga offers a delightful blend of artistic inspiration and coastal tranquility. One of the highlights of Olga is the artists' co-op, a gathering place for local artisans to showcase their talent. Here, you can browse through a diverse collection of handcrafted artworks, including paintings, sculptures, ceramics, and jewelry. The co-op not only provides a platform for artists to display their creations but also offers a unique opportunity to meet and engage with the creative minds behind the work. As you stroll through the village, you'll be captivated by the rustic charm of Olga, with its historic buildings, scenic gardens, and breathtaking views of the Salish Sea.

A short journey to Lopez Island leads you to the hidden gem of Watmough Bay. Tucked away from the more frequented areas of the island, this pristine bay offers a tranquil retreat for those seeking solace in nature. As you make your way to Watmough Bay, you'll encounter a winding road that takes you through lush forests and rolling farmlands, creating a sense of anticipation for what lies ahead. Upon arrival, you'll be greeted by a secluded beach of golden sand, gently lapped by the crystal-clear waters of the bay. The beach is perfect for a leisurely stroll, beachcombing for shells and treasures washed ashore, or simply sitting back and immersing yourself in the serenity of the surroundings. Bring along a picnic and find a shaded spot beneath the towering trees, where you can savor your meal while enjoying the panoramic views of the bay and its vibrant marine life.

For those with a thirst for history and maritime heritage, a visit to Shaw Island's lesser-known gem, the Shaw Island Historical Museum, is a must. Housed in a charming building that was once a general store, this museum offers a captivating journey through the island's intriguing past. Inside, you'll find an extensive collection of artifacts, photographs, and memorabilia that tell the story of Shaw Island and its inhabitants. Explore exhibits detailing the island's Native American heritage, early settlements, logging industry, and the crucial role of the maritime trade in shaping the island's history. Learn about the fascinating characters who played significant roles in the island's development, from the pioneers who braved the rugged terrain to the captains of the steamships that connected the island to the outside world. The museum's knowledgeable staff are eager to share their insights and stories, providing a deeper understanding of Shaw Island's rich heritage.

As you venture off the beaten path to explore these hidden gems, you'll discover a different side of the San Juan Islands. Olga's artistic spirit, Watmough Bay's pristine beauty, and the Shaw Island Historical Museum's fascinating history all contribute to the tapestry of experiences that make the San Juan Islands so unique.

In Olga, Orcas Island, the artistic energy permeates the village, creating an ambiance that is both inspiring and inviting. The artists' co-op is not only a place to admire and purchase unique creations but also a hub of creativity and collaboration. You might find yourself engrossed in a conversation with a painter, learning about their techniques and the stories behind their art. The co-op often hosts art workshops and events, providing opportunities for visitors to engage with the local arts community and even try their hand at creating their own masterpiece. As you stroll through Olga, take a moment to appreciate the historic Orcas Island Artworks, a converted strawberry barreling plant that now houses a collective of artists' studios and galleries. Step inside and witness firsthand the creative process in action as artists work on their latest projects. The scent of fresh paint and the buzz of artistic energy will ignite your own creative spark.

On Lopez Island, Watmough Bay is a hidden oasis that offers seclusion and serenity. Accessible via a scenic trail that winds through dense forest and open meadows, the journey to Watmough Bay itself is an experience worth savoring. As you meander along the path, the symphony of nature greets you with the melodious chirping of birds and the whispering of leaves in the gentle breeze. Upon reaching the bay, the sight of the expansive shoreline stretching out before you is simply breathtaking. Take off your shoes and feel the soft sand beneath your toes as you explore the beach, keeping an eye out for intricate seashells and colorful sea glass that adorn the shore. If you're lucky, you may even spot a majestic eagle soaring overhead or a playful seal popping up from the water. With no crowds or distractions, Watmough Bay provides an ideal setting for quiet reflection, meditation, or simply embracing the solitude of nature.

Shaw Island, often overshadowed by its larger neighbors, offers a hidden gem that beckons history enthusiasts and curious minds—the Shaw Island Historical Museum. Step inside this quaint museum, and you'll be transported back in time, gaining insight into the island's captivating past. The museum's exhibits showcase the island's Native American heritage, shedding light on the cultural traditions and deep connections to the land and sea. Explore artifacts that paint a vivid picture of early island life, from the tools used by settlers to the garments worn by the pioneers. Photographs and documents offer glimpses into the lives of the island's inhabitants throughout history, allowing you to connect with their stories and the challenges they faced. The museum's knowledgeable volunteers are passionate about preserving Shaw Island's heritage and are eager to share their knowledge, answering questions and providing context to deepen your understanding of the island's unique character.

Visiting these hidden gems and uncovering local secrets is an invitation to connect with the essence of the San Juan Islands. It's an opportunity to go beyond the surface-level attractions and delve into the heart of the community and the land. As you explore Olga's artistic spirit, Watmough Bay's natural beauty, and the Shaw Island Historical Museum's captivating exhibits, you'll gain a deeper appreciation for the richness and diversity that the San Juan Islands have to offer. These hidden gems are reminders that there is always more to discover and that true exploration goes beyond ticking off tourist destinations. Embrace the spirit of curiosity, wander off the beaten path, and let the San Juan Islands reveal their hidden treasures to you.

Off-the-Beaten-Path Day Trips:

Take a ferry to Sucia Island Marine State Park, a hidden gem with breathtaking sea caves, tide pools, and camping opportunities.

If you're seeking a truly secluded and awe-inspiring destination, a day trip to Sucia Island Marine State Park is an absolute must. Located just a short ferry ride away from the main islands, Sucia Island offers a pristine natural environment that will leave you breathless.

Upon arriving at Sucia Island, you'll immediately understand why it's often referred to as the "Gem of the San Juans." The island is a haven for outdoor enthusiasts, boasting an array of activities and stunning landscapes. One of the highlights of Sucia Island is its breathtaking sea caves, carved by centuries of tidal forces. Exploring these caves is a unique experience that will take you into a world of wonder and enchantment.

Tide pools dot the shoreline of Sucia Island, providing a fascinating opportunity to observe marine life up close. From colorful sea stars and anemones to tiny crabs and snails, these tide pools are teeming with biodiversity. Remember to tread carefully and observe from a respectful distance to ensure the preservation of this delicate ecosystem.

Camping on Sucia Island is an incredible way to extend your day trip into an overnight adventure. The island offers several campsites, each with its own unique charm and scenic beauty. Imagine falling asleep under a canopy of stars, surrounded by the soothing sounds of nature. Wake up to the gentle lapping of waves against the shore and witness a stunning sunrise over the Salish Sea. Camping on Sucia Island is an experience that will reconnect you with the natural world and leave you with cherished memories.

Embark on a day trip to Stuart Island, where you can hike to Turn Point Lighthouse and soak in panoramic views of the surrounding islands.

For those seeking solitude and breathtaking panoramic views, a day trip to Stuart Island is an excellent choice. Accessible by ferry, Stuart Island offers a serene and tranquil environment that feels worlds away from the hustle and bustle of everyday life.

One of the highlights of Stuart Island is the hike to Turn Point Lighthouse. As you trek through the island's picturesque trails, you'll be surrounded by lush greenery and the soothing sounds of nature. The lighthouse itself is a historic landmark that has guided mariners through the treacherous waters of Haro Strait for over a century. From the lighthouse, you'll be rewarded with sweeping vistas of the surrounding islands and the shimmering expanse of the Salish Sea. It's a truly breathtaking sight that will leave an indelible impression on your soul.

Apart from the hike to Turn Point Lighthouse, Stuart Island offers ample opportunities for exploration and relaxation. Take a leisurely stroll along the shoreline and let the waves wash away your worries. Enjoy a picnic amidst the island's serene beauty or find a peaceful spot to sit and contemplate life's wonders. Stuart Island is a place where time seems to slow down, allowing you to immerse yourself in the present moment and appreciate the simple joys of being in nature.

Explore the tranquil beauty of Jones Island State Park, accessible by private boat or kayak, offering scenic trails and a peaceful atmosphere.

If you're looking for a tranquil escape away from the crowds, a day trip to Jones Island State Park is an ideal choice. This hidden gem, accessible by private boat or kayak, offers a serene atmosphere and scenic trails that will transport you to a place of serenity and natural beauty.

As you approach Jones Island, you'll be greeted by its untouched shoreline, framed by towering evergreen trees. The park's network of trails allows you to explore the island's diverse ecosystems, from dense forests to pristine beaches. Take a leisurely hike along the trails, and you'll discover hidden coves, stunning viewpoints, and a rich tapestry of flora and fauna.

Jones Island is a paradise for birdwatchers, as it serves as an important nesting site for various seabirds and waterfowl. Keep your binoculars handy and be on the lookout for bald eagles soaring overhead, great blue herons wading in the shallows, and the melodic calls of songbirds echoing through the trees. The island's peaceful ambiance provides the perfect backdrop for observing and appreciating the wonders of the avian world.

One of the unique features of Jones Island is the solitude it offers. With limited visitor moorage and a small number of campsites, you're likely to find yourself in a tranquil oasis with minimal distractions. Whether you choose to spend your day exploring the trails, enjoying a picnic on the beach, or simply basking in the serenity of your surroundings, Jones Island will leave you feeling rejuvenated and connected to nature.

In conclusion, the San Juan Islands offer an abundance of off-the-beaten-path day trips that allow you to discover hidden gems and experience the untouched beauty of these Pacific Northwest wonders. From the sea caves of Sucia Island to the panoramic vistas of Stuart Island and the tranquil trails of Jones Island, each day trip presents a unique opportunity to immerse yourself in the natural splendor of the San Juan Islands. So, venture beyond the well-trodden paths, and let these off-the-beaten-path destinations captivate your heart and awaken your sense of adventure.

Uncovering Island History and Folklore:

Dive into the fascinating history of Lime Kiln Point State Park on San Juan Island, known as the "Whale Watch Park" due to its rich history of orca research.

Lime Kiln Point State Park, located on the western shore of San Juan Island, is not only renowned for its stunning coastal beauty but also for its significant role in the study and conservation of orcas, also known as killer whales. The park's history is intertwined with the remarkable efforts to understand these magnificent creatures and their behavior in the wild.

In the late 19th century, lime production was a thriving industry on San Juan Island. The park derives its name from the lime kilns that were used to convert limestone into lime for various applications. These kilns played a crucial role in the local economy, producing a high-quality lime used in construction and agriculture.

However, it wasn't until the mid-20th century that Lime Kiln Point gained recognition as a prime location for studying orcas. In the 1960s, researchers discovered that the waters surrounding the park served as a vital corridor for the Southern Resident Killer Whales, a distinct population of orcas that are now classified as endangered.

Today, Lime Kiln Point State Park is known as one of the best places in the world to observe these magnificent marine mammals from the shore. The park's rocky shoreline and strategic position provide visitors with a unique opportunity to witness orcas in their natural habitat, often coming remarkably close to the shore as they travel through the Haro Strait.

Visitors to the park can explore the network of trails that wind through the coastal forest, offering scenic views of the Salish Sea. The park's iconic lighthouse, built in 1919, stands as a testament to the maritime heritage of the region and provides a picturesque backdrop for whale watching enthusiasts.

Learn about the enigmatic story of the Pig War, a bloodless territorial dispute between the United States and Britain that took place on San Juan Island in the mid-19th century.

The Pig War, a peculiar conflict that unfolded on San Juan Island in the 1850s, stands as a testament to the complicated history between the United States and Britain and showcases a unique example of resolving disputes without bloodshed.

The origins of the Pig War can be traced back to the Treaty of Oregon, signed in 1846, which established the border between the United States and British North America (now Canada). The treaty left the ownership of several islands, including San Juan Island, in dispute. Both the United States and Britain claimed sovereignty over the island, leading to a tense situation.

In June 1859, a pig belonging to a British farmer on the island wandered into an American settler's garden, damaging crops. The American, Charles Griffin, decided to take matters into his own hands and shot the pig. The pig's owner, a British subject named Lyman Cutlar, demanded compensation for the loss of his prized pig. The incident quickly escalated into a heated confrontation between American and British authorities.

Word of the pig shooting reached higher authorities in both countries, triggering a military buildup on San Juan Island. Troops from both the United States and Britain were dispatched to the island, increasing tensions and raising the risk of armed conflict.

Despite the escalating situation, the commanders on the ground, Brigadier General William S. Harney for the United States and Captain George Pickett for Britain, exercised restraint and chose to avoid bloodshed. Known for their pragmatism, the two commanders engaged in a series of informal negotiations and agreements that prevented an armed confrontation.

The dispute ultimately reached the attention of their respective governments, who realized the need for a diplomatic resolution. In 1871, the matter was referred to arbitration by the German Emperor, Kaiser Wilhelm I. The arbitration resulted in a ruling in favor of the United States, establishing its sovereignty over San Juan Island.

The Pig War, despite its comical beginnings, had significant implications for the future of the San Juan Islands. The conflict highlighted the need for a clear border delineation and led to the eventual establishment of the International Boundary Commission, which surveyed and demarcated the boundary between the United States and Canada.

Today, visitors to San Juan Island can explore the remnants of the Pig War era. The English Camp and American Camp, established by the respective military forces during the dispute, offer a glimpse into the island's past. These historical sites provide interpretive displays, exhibits, and reconstructed buildings that shed light on the events that transpired during the Pig War.

Discover the legends and lore surrounding the Madrona Tree of Orcas Island, believed by some to possess mystical powers and spiritual significance.

Orcas Island, one of the largest islands in the San Juan archipelago, is home to a majestic tree that has captured the imagination and wonder of locals and visitors alike - the Madrona Tree. Known for its distinctive reddish-orange bark and graceful branches, the Madrona Tree holds a special place in the hearts of those who believe in its mystical powers and spiritual significance.

According to local legends, the Madrona Tree is considered a sacred tree and a symbol of strength and resilience. It is believed that the tree possesses healing properties, and its presence can bring a sense of peace and tranquility to those who encounter it. The Madrona Tree is also associated with purification and renewal, and some believe that it has the power to cleanse negative energy and bring about positive transformations.

The Madrona Tree has deep roots in the cultural heritage of the indigenous Coast Salish tribes who have inhabited the region for thousands of years. These tribes hold the Madrona Tree in high esteem, considering it a sacred tree that connects the physical and spiritual realms.

Visitors to Orcas Island can often find the Madrona Tree in secluded and serene locations, nestled among the island's forests and coastline. Its twisted branches and vibrant bark make it an enchanting sight, particularly during the golden hours of sunrise and sunset when its warm hues are accentuated.

Many people who encounter the Madrona Tree feel a sense of reverence and awe, drawn to its natural beauty and the sense of tranquility it exudes. Some even participate in rituals or meditative practices beneath its branches, seeking solace, inspiration, and a deeper connection to nature.

As you explore Orcas Island, keep an eye out for these magnificent trees. Whether you embrace the legends and lore surrounding the Madrona Tree or simply appreciate its natural beauty, encountering these majestic beings can be a transformative experience, reminding us of the interconnectedness of all living things and the power of the natural world to inspire and heal.

By following these insider recommendations, you'll gain a deeper understanding of the San Juan Islands and uncover experiences that go beyond the well-trodden paths. Whether it's visiting lesser-explored islands, immersing yourself in local folklore, or seeking out hidden gems, these insider tips will add a layer of depth and authenticity to your journey. Get ready to create unforgettable memories as you explore the San Juan Islands with the knowledge and insights of those who know it best.

Chapter 10: Planning Your Return

After experiencing the enchanting San Juan Islands, you'll likely find yourself yearning to return to this captivating destination. In this chapter, we provide guidance on how to make the most of your future visits, ensuring that you continue to create lasting memories in this island paradise.

Reflecting on Your Experience:

Taking a moment to reflect on your journey through the San Juan Islands allows you to appreciate the depth of your experiences and gain valuable insights that will shape your future visits. It's a chance to connect with the highlights, the moments that touched your soul, and the activities that brought you immense joy. By delving into these reflections, you can create a roadmap for future adventures that align with your passions and desires.

Begin by recalling the highlights of your previous trip. What stands out in your memory? Was it the breathtaking views from the summit of Mount Constitution on Orcas Island? Or perhaps it was the exhilaration of spotting a pod of orcas gracefully swimming alongside your kayak? Reflect on the awe-inspiring moments that left an indelible mark on your heart.

Consider the activities that brought you joy during your time in the San Juan Islands. Did you find solace in exploring the tranquil hiking trails, immersing yourself in the pristine beauty of nature? Maybe you reveled in the local culinary scene, savoring fresh seafood delicacies paired with locally crafted wines. Identify the activities that resonated with you on a personal level, as they hold the key to shaping your future visits.

As you reflect, think about the emotions evoked during your time in the islands. Did you experience a sense of wonder as you observed the intricate dance of sea lions in their natural habitat? Did you feel a deep connection to the rhythm of island life, a sense of peace and contentment? These emotional responses provide valuable insights into the aspects of the San Juan Islands that resonate with you most profoundly.

Use these reflections as a guide for shaping your future visits to the San Juan Islands. Consider how you can amplify the moments that touched your soul and incorporate more of the activities that brought you joy. If you found solace in the island's natural beauty, plan to explore new hiking trails, discover hidden beaches, or engage in wildlife encounters that align with your interests. If the local culture and cuisine captured your heart, seek out new farm-to-table restaurants, attend cultural events, or participate in hands-on workshops that allow you to immerse yourself in the island's vibrant community.

Seasonal Highlights and Upcoming Events:

The San Juan Islands offer a wealth of seasonal highlights and events that ensure there's something captivating to experience throughout the year. Understanding these seasonal attractions will allow you to plan your next visit with precision, ensuring you don't miss out on the unique wonders that each season brings.

In the spring, the islands burst to life with vibrant blooms and rejuvenating energy. If you have a fondness for nature's colorful displays, the San Juan Islands' blooming wildflowers are a sight to behold. Explore the picturesque landscapes adorned with delicate wildflowers, including camas, lupine, and Indian paintbrush. Delight in the fragrant scents and vibrant hues as you embark on scenic hikes or leisurely strolls through meadows and coastal trails.

As summer arrives, the San Juan Islands become a hub for incredible wildlife encounters. Migrating whales, including majestic orcas, grace the surrounding waters, making it an opportune time for thrilling whale-watching excursions. Witness these magnificent creatures in their natural habitat, as they breach and play in the ocean waves. Keep an eye out for other marine wildlife such as seals, sea lions, and porpoises that frequent the archipelago during this season.

In the autumn months, the San Juan Islands transform into a tapestry of stunning fall foliage. The lush green landscapes transition into a captivating display of warm reds, fiery oranges, and golden hues. Take scenic drives or leisurely bike rides through the islands, immersing yourself in the natural beauty and serenity of the changing seasons. Capture photographs of the picturesque landscapes and relish in the tranquility that accompanies this time of year.

To enhance your experience in the San Juan Islands, it is essential to stay informed about upcoming events and festivals. The islands come alive with local festivities, cultural celebrations, and outdoor concerts that add a vibrant touch to your island experience. Immerse yourself in the lively atmosphere of music festivals, art fairs, and food markets, where you can indulge in local delicacies and interact with the welcoming island community. From the famous Friday Harbor Fourth of July Parade to the Orcas Island Chamber

Music Festival, there's always an event to celebrate and participate in.

To stay updated on the latest happenings, connect with local tourism boards, visit the official websites of the San Juan Islands, and follow social media accounts dedicated to island events. Plan your visit around these exciting events, allowing yourself to fully immerse in the dynamic and enriching island culture.

Creating an Itinerary:

Building upon your previous experience in the San Juan Islands, crafting a well-rounded itinerary for your future visit allows you to continue your exploration and create a new set of cherished memories. Here are some tips to help you plan your itinerary:

Revisiting Favorite Spots:

Consider returning to the places that captivated you during your previous visit. Whether it's a breathtaking viewpoint, a secluded beach, or a charming coastal town, revisiting these spots can evoke a sense of nostalgia while allowing you to see them through fresh eyes. Take note of any changes or developments since your last visit, as the islands are constantly evolving.

Exploring Different Islands:

The San Juan archipelago comprises several islands, each with its own unique character and attractions. If you focused on one or two islands during your previous trip, consider expanding your horizons by exploring other islands that you haven't yet experienced. Visit Orcas Island for its stunning landscapes and charming village, venture to Lopez Island for its tranquil atmosphere and picturesque farmland, or discover the historical sites and vibrant community of San Juan Island. Each island offers a distinct flavor and a wealth of new discoveries.

Incorporating New Activities:

While revisiting favorite activities can be enjoyable, don't hesitate to seek out new adventures that the San Juan Islands have to offer. Whether it's embarking on a kayaking expedition to explore hidden coves and sea caves, joining a guided wildlife tour to witness orcas or seals in their natural habitat, or trying your hand at fishing to catch a delectable salmon, embracing new activities will provide fresh perspectives and exciting experiences.

Unearthing Hidden Gems:

The San Juan Islands are filled with hidden gems waiting to be discovered. These could be lesser-known trails with breathtaking views, secluded beaches where you can find tranquility, or off-the-beaten-path attractions that showcase the islands' cultural heritage. Engage with locals, seek recommendations from fellow travelers, or consult travel resources to uncover these hidden treasures. These hidden gems often offer a deeper connection to the islands, immersing you in their unique essence.

Embracing Serendipity:

While planning your itinerary is important, leave room for spontaneity and unexpected adventures. Serendipitous encounters and impromptu explorations often lead to the most memorable experiences. Allow yourself to wander through charming towns, strike up conversations with locals, and follow your instincts when something catches your eye. Embrace the joy of discovering the unknown and let the San Juan Islands surprise you once again.

By building upon your previous experience, incorporating new elements, and being open to the unexpected, your well-rounded itinerary will ensure a fulfilling and enriching future visit to the San Juan Islands. Embrace the opportunity to deepen your connection to this captivating destination as you uncover its hidden wonders.

Exploring Further:

The San Juan Islands serve as a captivating introduction to the broader Pacific Northwest region, which offers a wealth of natural wonders, cultural hubs, and breathtaking landscapes waiting to be discovered. In this section, we provide resources and suggestions for expanding your horizons and embarking on further exploration beyond the San Juan Islands.

Vancouver Island:

Just a short ferry ride away from the San Juan Islands, Vancouver Island beckons with its own unique charm. Explore the charming city of Victoria, with its British colonial architecture and vibrant harbor. Discover the island's diverse ecosystems, from the old-growth forests of Cathedral Grove to the rugged coastline of Pacific Rim National Park. Engage in thrilling outdoor activities such as hiking, whale watching, or kayaking in the island's pristine waters.

Gulf Islands:

Situated between the San Juan Islands and Vancouver Island, the Gulf Islands offer a serene and tranquil escape. Each island in this archipelago has its own character, offering a slower pace of life, picturesque landscapes, and a thriving arts scene. Visit Salt Spring Island, known for its vibrant artisan community and local markets. Explore Pender Island's stunning beaches and hiking trails. Experience the serene beauty of Galiano Island, where nature and tranquility blend harmoniously.

Olympic Peninsula:

Venturing to the mainland, the Olympic Peninsula awaits with its dramatic coastline, ancient rainforests, and towering mountains. Discover Olympic National Park, a UNESCO World Heritage site, boasting diverse ecosystems ranging from rugged beaches to alpine meadows. Hike through moss-laden rainforests, soak in hot springs, or marvel at the awe-inspiring vistas from Hurricane Ridge. Don't miss the picturesque coastal town of Port Townsend, known for its Victorian architecture and vibrant arts community.

Seattle and Puget Sound:

A visit to the Pacific Northwest wouldn't be complete without experiencing the dynamic city of Seattle and the surrounding Puget Sound region. Immerse yourself in the city's vibrant neighborhoods, including Pike Place Market, the Space Needle, and the bustling waterfront. Explore the rich cultural scene, from world-class museums to lively music venues. Embark on a scenic ferry ride to the charming waterfront towns of Bainbridge Island or Whidbey Island, where stunning landscapes and local charm await.

Cascade Mountains:

For outdoor enthusiasts and nature lovers, the Cascade Mountains offer an abundance of opportunities for adventure. Experience the majesty of Mount Rainier National Park, with its towering peak, lush meadows, and pristine alpine lakes. Discover the enchanting landscapes of North Cascades National Park, known as the "American

Alps," with its rugged peaks, glaciers, and pristine wilderness. Engage in hiking, mountain biking, skiing, or simply bask in the tranquility of nature's grandeur.

As you delve into further exploration of the Pacific Northwest, embrace the diversity and beauty that this region has to offer. Each destination presents its own unique experiences, whether it's immersing yourself in the vibrant city life or communing with nature in pristine wilderness. Expand your horizons and continue your journey of discovery, uncovering the captivating tapestry of the Pacific Northwest.

Delving Deeper into History and Culture:

To gain a deeper understanding of the San Juan Islands' rich history and culture, immersing yourself in suggested reading materials will be a rewarding endeavor. These resources offer captivating stories, historical accounts, and local folklore that shed light on the islands' past, enabling you to connect more intimately with the land and its people. Here are some recommendations to enrich your knowledge and appreciation for the islands' heritage:

"The Pig War: Standoff at Griffin Bay" by Mike Vouri:

Delve into the fascinating history of the Pig War, a bloodless border dispute between the United States and Britain that occurred on San Juan Island in 1859. This book explores the events leading up to the standoff and provides insight into the island's role in the broader historical context.

"The Lummi Indians of Northwest Washington" by Robert J. Hefner:

Learn about the Lummi people, one of the indigenous groups who have inhabited the San Juan Islands for generations.

This book offers a comprehensive exploration of their history, culture, and enduring traditions. Gain a deeper appreciation for their connection to the land, their artistic expressions, and their contributions to the region.

"San Juan Islands: A Guide to Exploring the Great Outdoors" by Tom Kirkendall and Vicky Spring:

This guidebook not only provides practical information for outdoor activities but also delves into the natural and cultural history of the San Juan Islands. Learn about the geological formations, native plants, and wildlife that make these islands a unique ecological hotspot.

"The Pig War Islands: The San Juans of Northwest Washington State and Their Role in International Relations" by Terry L. Ommen:

Explore the intricate history of the San Juan Islands and their significant role in international relations. This book examines the complex dynamics between the United States and Britain during the Pig War and analyzes the political implications of the dispute.

"Voices of the Islands: History and Memory on San Juan, Orcas, and Lopez Islands" by John T. Williams:

Through oral histories and personal accounts, this book provides a compelling narrative of the islands' history as recounted by local residents. Gain insight into the experiences, challenges, and triumphs of the people who have shaped the San Juan Islands over the years.

By engaging with these suggested reading materials, you will deepen your knowledge of the San Juan Islands' past and foster a greater appreciation for their cultural heritage. As you embark on future visits, you will have a heightened understanding of the land's significance and a more profound connection to the communities that call these islands home.

As you plan your return to the San Juan Islands, remember to keep an open mind, allowing serendipity to guide your experiences. Embrace the opportunity to delve deeper into the wonders of this remarkable destination, creating memories that will last a lifetime.

Conclusion

As we conclude our San Juan Islands Travel Guide, we invite you to reflect on the remarkable journey you've just taken through this Pacific Northwest paradise. Throughout the chapters, we have unveiled the hidden gems, explored the major islands, ventured to lesser-known destinations, and immersed ourselves in the rich culture and history of this archipelago.

The San Juan Islands offer a captivating blend of natural beauty, outdoor adventures, cultural experiences, and culinary delights. From the majestic landscapes of Orcas Island to the charming streets of Friday Harbor on San Juan Island, and the tranquil shores of Lopez Island, each island presents its own unique allure and endless opportunities for exploration.

Whether you're seeking an outdoor adventure, a cultural immersion, or simply a peaceful retreat, the San Juan Islands have it all. Engage in kayaking or boating adventures, hike through pristine forests, witness awe-inspiring wildlife, and discover the stories that shaped the islands' past. Delight your taste buds with farm-fresh cuisine, savor local flavors, and support the vibrant arts and crafts scene.

The San Juan Islands' pristine beauty and unspoiled landscapes remind us of the importance of preserving and protecting these natural treasures. As you embark on your journey, we encourage you to practice responsible tourism, leaving no trace and respecting the delicate ecosystems and local communities that call these islands home.

Whether you're a nature enthusiast, history buff, art lover, or simply someone seeking tranquility and rejuvenation, the San Juan Islands have something to offer every traveler. As you depart these captivating shores, may the memories you've made and the experiences you've had stay with you, reminding you of the incredible beauty and diversity that exists within our world.

We hope that this travel guide has served as a valuable resource, equipping you with the knowledge and inspiration to embark on your own San Juan Islands adventure. From the moment you step foot on these islands, you'll be captivated by their charm, and we have no doubt that you'll leave with a piece of your heart forever embedded in the beauty of the San Juan Islands.

So, what are you waiting for? Start planning your journey to this enchanting archipelago, and let the San Juan Islands work their magic on you. Uncover the hidden gems, forge unforgettable memories, and embrace the natural wonders that await in Washington's beloved island paradise. The San Juan Islands are waiting to be discovered by you. Bon voyage!

Made in the USA
Monee, IL
22 January 2024